Online and Telephone Counselling

A Practitioner's Guide

By Kenneth Kelly
and
Rory Lees-Oakes

Edited by Sarah Carr

'This book would not have been possible without the editing skills of Sarah Carr from Carr Consultancy.'

ISBN: 978-0-9957696-6-3 (paperback)
ISBN: 978-0-9957696-7-0 (ebook)

Contents

How to Use This Book

This book comes with a free online companion course and a template library, where you can download paperwork templates and examples for your online practice.

Get access to the companion course by visiting this link:
counsellingtutor.com/online

Be excited; be very excited! You hold in your hand a book that can help you make the move from face-to-face to remote working, and there has never been a better time to make this transition.

Online and telephone therapy is experiencing a period of rapid growth. More and more, clients are trusting that remote contact is a way to overcome a range of issues, and the evidence suggests that clients are finding the online process convenient and effective.

You need only look to the growth in tele-medicine services to see how technology is changing the way that help can be delivered. Tens of millions of pounds are being invested into remote medical services, with the aim of helping more people – more quickly and at a lower cost.

Traditionally, as face-to-face therapists, we serve our local community within a certain radius of our practice. Running a successful practice means we hire a counselling room or set aside part of our home in which to see clients, and we rely on our client to make their way to us. Online therapy holds the promise of breaking down geographical boundaries, allowing therapists to work with more clients, save travel time and reduce overheads.

However, there can be a darker, unseen side to working remotely. Things can – and do – go wrong. When an issue fractures the therapeutic relationship in a face-to-face setting, we get a chance to repair this with our client. When such issues arise online, it can play out very differently, as we have no control over the environment. When online therapy goes wrong, it can have devastating effects for both you and the client.

This book was written to help you learn the necessary core competences to work safely and ethically with your clients online, through email, via telephone and by text.

Note: for ease of writing, when we use the phrase 'online counselling' or 'online therapy' in this book, we mean it as a generic term to apply to video, telephone, text and email counselling.

Disclaimer

Will this book enable me to be an online counsellor? The short answer to this question is: 'No.' Before you rush to claim a refund, please allow us to explain.

As counsellors, we are required to be congruent, transparent and ethical. We wanted to outline what this book 'is not' upfront to save you the time of reading the entire book only to find that your expectations have not been met.

This book is not a qualification; it is a guide that outlines the principles, theory and application of online, telephone, text and email therapy. In the same way as you can't learn to become a counsellor by reading a book, you also can't qualify as an online practitioner by just reading and turning pages.

To call yourself an online therapist, you will need to undertake a formal training course. Ethical bodies around the world differ in their requirements regarding qualifications to work online; it is recommended that you look to your own ethical body for direction on the requirements in your country and jurisdiction.

Our author team is based in the United Kingdom and so we refer to the British Association of Counselling and Psychotherapy (BACP) competences for telephone and e-counselling. The BACP requires therapists to undertake a formal training course with a minimum of 80 hours of guided learning and experiential work that is mapped to a set of core competences.

What Is the Value of Owning and Reading This Book?

That's simple. This book is a guide that gives you the building blocks you will need to work ethically and safely with your clients online. All that is missing is the experiential aspect, where you practise the learning and get peer feedback.

Buying a car does not qualify a person to drive safely even if they have read the Highway Code. To drive safely and within the law takes practice, trial and plenty of error. Think back to your own first few driving experiences. If they are anything like ours, you may recall anxiety, gear-crunching, stalling and maybe even a tiny bump.

Now compare that to your driving practice today. You probably drive with unconscious competence. In other words, your driving has become second nature through practice.

Think of this book as your shiny new car: it is exactly what you need to get yourself working online safely and ethically, but you also need to gain some practice and feedback in order to be fully competent.

It is unethical for us as counsellors to crunch gears, stall or work anxiously with live clients. We need first to sharpen our competence so we can serve our clients with confidence, and work ethically and safely.

Interested in Formal Training?

Our team at Counselling Tutor runs a formal course, Online and Telephone Counselling, with a start date every month. The course is self-paced, meaning you can do it whenever fits for you. And it is delivered online – so you can join from wherever you are in the world. Our course provides over 100 hours of guided tuition and experiential work, with regular live online events to clarify your learning and allow you to ask any questions.

The very book you hold in your hand was written to underpin our formal training course. And if you do decide to join our course, you will get the price you paid for this book discounted from your enrolment fee.

We have helped thousands of therapists from around the world to transition from face-to-face to online work. So, if you are interested in getting more formal training to work online, please visit our website www.counsellingtutor.com

Tips on Reading This Book

> We recommend that you work through the book in order, completing all elements as you go. Any example documents – which are put forward not as best practice, but as guides that you can use and adapt in your own practice, if useful – are shaded in light-grey, like this.

Each section of each chapter includes two boxes at the end, which look like this:

> *Questions to reflect on*
> -
> -
> -

Do take the time to reflect on the questions and to complete the tasks in each chapter section, as doing so will greatly enhance your learning from reading this book, helping you gain wisdom rather than just knowledge.

Online and Telephone Counselling

Chapter 1

Getting Started with Online Counselling

Your Online Mindset

'We see the world not as it is, but as we are.' – Anais Nin

As counsellors, we learn how 'frame of reference' influences how we and others see the world. We reference our past knowledge and experience, and project a 'reality' that matches our beliefs, culture and heritage. We call our interpretation our 'truth'.

We understand that one person's truth can differ greatly from another's, and that our training helps us accept a client's frame of reference, without judgement.

Of course, much of counselling training deals with self-development, and we are called upon to challenge our own beliefs and perceived truths in order to grow and become more fluid in our worldly outlook.

Working remotely requires us to use some form of technology to connect with our client. Ordinarily, in face-to-face counselling, the use of email, texting applications, video software or telephone would not play a major part in the therapeutic relationship. Before embarking on online therapy, we must examine and challenge our own beliefs and past experiences of working with technology so as not to colour the therapeutic relationship with our own frame of reference.

Take a moment to consider what your past relationship with technology feels like. What feelings come up for you when you think about learning something new on a computer? Can you recall a time when you became frustrated, scared, anxious or confused by technology?

From our own experience, we recognise that there are times when technology felt like a foreign language to us, and we would become so anxious and frustrated that often we would just walk away. We would feel we just couldn't do it, feeling we had failed, and feeling angry with ourselves for 'being so stupid'.

Your relationship with technology may be very different, but it needs exploring all the same. I encourage you to reflect on your current and past relationships with technology, and to share them with a peer or your supervisor, as the outcomes can be illuminating. By sharing with another person, we gain more insight. Through feedback, we can better understand that which is perhaps unseen by us. By understanding your relationship with technology, you are empowered and can avoid unconscious contamination of the client's journey.

Your online mindset will form part of the therapeutic relationship, whether consciously or unconsciously. In training, we study how transference and countertransference can be present in the counselling relationship without either client or counsellor being aware of it. In the same way, our relationship with technology can be projected onto the client without us being consciously aware of this. For example, if we are fearful of technology, this can leak out and shake the confidence of the client. Or, if we are over-confident, then we run the risk of leaving the client feeling inferior or stupid as they can't follow or understand.

The good news is that you don't need to be a computer whizz to work online; the tools and applications are pretty easy to master with practice. This exercise on mindset is not about your competence using these tools, but rather about your 'frame of reference' related to working with and using technology in general.

The very first point to remember when preparing to work online is to gear up your 'online mindset' – in other words, to give equal value to your online work and your face-to-face work, so that you can feel positively about this way of working yourself, and transmit your enthusiasm to your clients. Online counselling is different from face-to-face counselling, but it is by no means second-best. By valuing the way you work, you are in turn valuing your client and the choice they have made to work with you remotely. Competence and care are bywords for professional practice. You need to invest in and commit yourself to this way of working so that the client can make the same investment.

Initial Contact

The process of working online with a client usually starts with the client reaching out to you via email, telephone or an online form on your website.

How we reply to this initial contact needs careful consideration. The potential client is starting a conversation with us, and we need to respond in a way that both continues that conversation and gives the person the details they need to make an informed decision on whether online counselling would be a good fit for them.

The best way to do this is to ask if you can email them with your details. An example of an initial contact response might be as follows (you are welcome to use this, tweaking it to fit your own style and practice):

 You can download this example from within the free online companion course by visiting counsellingtutor.com/online

Initial Contact Response

Hello [potential client's name]

Thank you for taking the time to get in touch with me. I hear you are looking to explore some difficulties that you have been dealing with for some time, and you are wondering whether online counselling may be an option for you.

I have attached a Word document outlining the service I offer, along with some information about what online counselling is and how it works. The document has a section outlining a working agreement, as well as a few questions. Your answers will help me better understand your situation.

If you feel the information fits with what you are looking for, please complete the form and return it to me. I will then review the information you have provided to check whether my skills will match your requirements. I will reply to you within 48 hours of receiving your completed agreement form.

If you cannot download the attached file or have any difficulty opening it, please let me know and I will send it in another format. And if you have any questions about the form, again do please tell me, and I will do my best to answer them.

I look forward to your reply.

With warm wishes

[Counsellor's name]

It may be harder for clients to get a full picture of what's on offer when working online, as they don't get the opportunity to physically enter the building and talk face-to-face with the practitioner. Producing an agreement form can be a really useful way to surmount this, and you can attach this to your initial contact response, asking the client to complete it and return it to you.

The reasons for using an agreement form in online therapy are as follows:

- It gives clients an overview of what is on offer from a therapeutic perspective.
- It outlines what online counselling is.
- It gives the client a choice about the type of communication technology available so they can choose the option that is best suited to them.

- It normalises the idea that online therapy is a legitimate way of engaging with a therapist, which helps both to instil confidence and to develop an online mindset in the client.

We include an example below; this is one written by a person-centred therapist, but can be adapted to fit you, your modality, your practice and your way of working. The agreement form describes your way of working, answers common questions about online counselling, and elicits some additional information from the client to help you check whether your skills and experience will be a good fit for their needs.

Please note that neither the initial contact response nor the agreement form is a formal contract.

 You can download this example from within the free online companion course by visiting counsellingtutor.com/online

Agreement Form

About me
My name is [counsellor's name]. I am qualified in person-centred counselling and I am a registered member of [professional body]. I adhere to the [your ethical framework]; more information on this can be found at [professional body's website].

What is person-centred counselling?
I find the person-centred approach fits my own philosophy as

it has at its very core an unshakeable belief that all people are good. Person-centred counsellors believe that each and every person can become a more fully functioning person – and will do so if they are given the correct conditions. The underpinning principles of the person-centred approach are focused on the counsellor being honest, non-judgemental and fully accepting, whilst being integrated in the relationship and allowing the client to lead and set the pace. I aim to offer these conditions as best as I can during our relationship.

What is online counselling?

Online counselling is a way for you to engage in counselling using internet technology such as Zoom, email, online chat or webcam video link. You direct your counselling by selecting the method of communication you feel most comfortable with. You choose the time, the place and the pace of your counselling to suit your needs.

How it works

Webcam counselling

Zoom is a way for you to see your counsellor face-to-face from your computer while engaging in therapy. You will be guided through setting up your own encrypted Zoom account and you will meet your counsellor on Zoom at a time that you have previously arranged. Sessions are 50 minutes in length. Being able to see your counsellor gives you more of the benefits you get from face-to-face counselling but with the convenience of online therapy. By talking, you hear tone of voice (which is a way to convey empathy); and with video, you see nonverbal communications, such as facial expressions.

Email counselling

Counselling by email offers you the opportunity to consider what you wish to say before you send it, as well as time between exchanges to reflect on the information you have received. You will be guided on how to set up a secure email account and will then have a set number of email contacts with your counsellor. Email counselling is also sometimes used between more structured sessions, such as online chat, telephone or webcam counselling. A consideration of email counselling is the time delay between your mail and the return mail; this makes email counselling ineffective when your situation is urgent.

Telephone counselling

This is similar to webcam counselling as it happens through the Zoom system, or via a handset, but without the visual aspects. You can choose to remain anonymous and the conversation is encrypted if held on Zoom. An advantage of telephone counselling is that nonverbal communication can be carried in your tone of voice or the pace of speech, which can be picked up by your counsellor. A disadvantage of telephone counselling is that you need a private room where you will not be overheard. Online counselling offers certain benefits, but there are also limitations that are worth bearing in mind when deciding which type of therapy will best suit your needs.

Online-chat counselling

If you choose the online chat room, you will be directed to a secure login page that takes you to an encrypted area where you meet your counsellor at a time that was prearranged beforehand. Your session is 50 minutes long and a transcript is available afterwards, allowing you to review what both you and your counsellor said. This gives you the opportunity to clarify any uncertainties you may have from your session, and also leaves you with something to go back to as you process the information. You do not need a webcam for this counselling and you can choose to remain anonymous if you wish.

Online counselling offers certain benefits, but there are also limitations that are worth bearing in mind when deciding which type of therapy will best suit your needs.

Benefits
- Counselling therapy takes place from your own home (or other chosen place) – meaning that you don't have to travel.
- Secure encryption software offers confidentiality and peace of mind.
- There is no chance that you may be seen entering the counsellor's practice.
- When using email or online chat, you can review what you are saying before sending it.
- Therapy happens at a time, place and pace that suit you.
- You may find it easier to express your feelings by writing them down.
- Access to counselling may be more immediate.
- You can choose the technology you feel is best for you: telephone, email, live chat or webcam.

Things to consider
- Are you comfortable using internet technology?

- Do you feel you can express your feelings effectively using words?
- Do you feel your situation is too complex to discuss via the internet?
- Is there a computer terminal that you can use privately without interruption?
- Text communication can sometimes be open to misunderstanding.
- There are no nonverbal cues or body language for you or the counsellor to read; this can lead to misunderstanding.

Confidentiality and security

Online counselling takes place within a secure, encrypted environment to offer you confidentiality and safety. Email correspondence is encouraged through a secure mail server; you will be instructed on how to set up a confidential email account for your counselling therapy. Telephone and webcam counselling take advantage of the encrypted services offered by Zoom, and your counsellor will guide you through setting up a free account for your therapy.

You can read my privacy policy regarding how information you supply is handled by visiting this link: [your website address]

The information shared with me is held in strict confidence and all electronically stored information is stored on a password-protected drive.

In adherence with [your ethical framework], I am obliged to break confidentiality if you disclose involvement in or knowledge of an act of terrorism, money laundering or drugs trafficking. In addition, I have an agency policy to report instances of harm to self or to others, and I do have a legal obligation to report harm or abuse of a minor or vulnerable adult.

Email correspondence is encouraged through a secure mail server such as Hushmail, to prevent your messages being intercepted and read by a third party. I will explain how to set up a confidential email account for your counselling therapy.

The content of your emails will not be communicated with anyone except for the purposes of supervision of my practice. When elements of our sessions are taken to supervision, no identifying information (such as your name) is used. My supervisor also follows the same procedures for confidentiality as I have outlined.

Audio or video counselling takes advantage of the encrypted services offered by Zoom. If you choose this method of counselling, I will guide you through setting up a free account for your therapy. You do not need a webcam to use Zoom counselling.

At the end of our counselling agreement, copies of our exchanges will be stored electronically on a password-protected drive for a period of [length of time, depending on your insurance policy]. After this time, the information will be deleted and any paper documents will be shredded.

In addition, if at any point during the counselling you are in need of emergency care, I may ask for your consent to contact your GP, or recommend avenues of support other than online counselling.

In an emergency

Online counselling is not sufficient support if you feel you are in crisis. Signs of crisis may be feelings of wanting to take your own life, or to harm yourself or someone else. In this case, please contact your nearest accident and emergency (A&E) department and ask to someone from the crisis team. You could also call the Samaritans on 116 123 or email jo@samaritans.org

Conditions of counselling

As I aim to offer confidentiality regarding the content of our sessions, I would ask that you do the same by not sharing any of the content of our sessions with any third party.

If you have any questions regarding the content of this agreement, or would like further information, please email me at [email address] or call me on [phone number].

Please provide the information requested below and then return this agreement form to me.

Full name:

Date of Birth:

Address:

Telephone:

Email:

Preferred means of contact:

Best time to contact:

Emergency contact number in case of technology breakdown:

What are you looking to address in counselling?

Are you currently having or have you had counselling in the past?

History of previous or existing medical/psychiatric conditions or hospital admissions:

Any medical appointments due and what for:

History of violence, overdose or self-harm:

GP contact details:

Please 'sign electronically' here with your name if you agree to working to the points within this agreement:

Please return this document by email to counsellor@ mycounsellingpractice.co.uk

I aim to contact you via your preferred contact method within 48 hours of receipt of this form with further information regarding your counselling.

Let the client choose

Do remember, when moving to online or telephone counselling (especially if you are not currently offering face-to-face sessions), that you are effectively making a new offer to the client. Avoid saying: 'I am going online from next week. I will send you a link to my online meeting room.' Instead, you need to respect the client's autonomy, exploring how the client feels about you in effect entering their home (if that is where they plan to be for the session), and what they think about working remotely online. Use the agreement form as a basis of making a new offer and let the client decide.

Avoid negativity

Having an online mindset means that you give equal value to your online work as you do to your face-to-face work. You need to invest yourself in this way of working so the client can make the same investment. Be aware that your client may be nervous or unsure of online therapy, and so avoid saying things yourself that could fuel this reticence, for example:

- ✗ 'It's OK but not as good as face-to-face.'
- ✗ 'I could do so much more if we were in the same room.'
- ✗ 'The technology gets in the way.'
- ✗ 'This is not the way I usually work.'

Instead, you need to speak and behave in a way that simultaneously allows the client choice, recognises and empathises with their view of working online and/or by telephone, and promotes the idea that you see this as an equal alternative in which you are confident and competent.

This includes becoming really comfortable and familiar yourself with the technology required (e.g. video-conferencing software, such as Zoom), believing that you can achieve this (even if you don't already have experience of working with it), and supporting the client to learn to do so themselves.

Questions to reflect on
- Does the technology add to your power in the eyes of the client?
- What are your attitudes to practising online?
- What do you need to do or say to normalise an online way of working?
- Are you giving the client the autonomy and information to choose whether they wish to work online and with you?

Tasks to complete
- Find a buddy for practice (for example, a peer at college or a colleague in your counselling agency).
- Create your own initial contact response (using our example as a basis if helpful) that reflects your own voice and style, and check it out with your buddy.
- Formulate your own agreement form (again drawing on our example if you wish) to attach to your email, and ask your buddy for their views.
- Try out the technology you plan to use (e.g. Zoom) by yourself and with your buddy, to build your comfort and familiarity with this (just as you needed to practise with your audio-recorder during skills practice while training).
- Reflect on your own online mindset (perhaps through journaling about this to explore your thoughts and feelings, and talking to others).

Relationship with Technology

As mentioned, it is important to consider your relationship with technology before offering any therapy online. How confident do you feel using email, video-conferencing software (e.g. Zoom) and smartphones? You need to be really honest with yourself and audit your technological skill set. Consider how confident you would be teaching a client to set up an email account or helping them download webinar software onto their device.

You may find it useful to refer to the following Glossary of Technology Terms (CCPA, 2019: 26–30) to check how comfortable you feel with the relevant language.

 You can download this example from within the free online companion course by visiting counsellingtutor.com/online

Glossary of Technology Terms

Apps
An abbreviation for 'application'. It's a piece of software that can run via a web browser or even offline on your computer, mobile phone, tablet or any other electronic device. Apps may or may not have a connection to the internet.

Asynchronous text-based counselling
In this modality of counselling, the mode of communication is text. The client and counsellor do not have to be sitting at their

computer at the same time, resulting in a stretched timeframe in which interaction occurs.

Backup policy

A pre-defined, set schedule whereby information from business applications such as Oracle, Microsoft SQL, email server databases and user files is copied to disk and/or tape to ensure data recoverability in the event of accidental data deletion, corrupted information or some kind of a system outage. It can also be an organisation's procedures and rules for ensuring that adequate amounts and types of backups are made, including suitably frequent testing of the process for restoring the original production system from the backup copies.

Backup systems

The process in which the state, files and data of a computer system are duplicated, to be used as a backup or data substitute when the primary system data is corrupted, deleted or lost.

Cloud storage

'Cloud storage' refers to online space that you can use to store your data. The simplest type of cloud storage occurs when users upload files and folders on their computers or mobile devices to an internet server. The uploaded files serve as a backup in case the original files are damaged or lost. Using a cloud server permits the user to download files to other devices when needed. The files are typically protected by encryption and are accessed by the user with login credentials and password. The files are always available to the user, as long as the user has an internet connection to view or retrieve them.

Data removal app

An app that allows you to securely remove data and documents from any of your devices. This can be done in person or remotely, in case the device is lost or stolen.

Disinhibition

People may behave differently online/when using other media from the ways in which they might interact in face-to-face situations. They may disclose information more quickly than they would in face-to-face situations. They may also be uninhibited in their expressions of emotions (e.g. more insensitive or angry). These differences in behaviour may be influenced by the following features of the online environment:

- having the sense of being anonymous and invisible
- not seeing (and therefore not experiencing) other people's reactions to what is said
- experiencing an absence of external authority in the online/other media environment
- not experiencing others as 'real'.

Encryption

Data encryption translates data into another form, or code, so that only people with access to a secret key (formally called a 'decryption key') or password can read it.

Firewalls

A network security system that monitors and controls incoming and outgoing network traffic based on predetermined security rules. A firewall typically establishes a barrier between a trusted internal network and untrusted outside network, such as the internet.

Hardware

The physical parts or components of a computer, such as the monitor, keyboard, computer data storage, graphic card, sound card and motherboard. Hardware is directed by the software to execute any command or instruction.

Live chat

A real-time transmission of text messages from sender to receiver. Chat messages are generally short in order to enable other participants to respond quickly.

Malware

'Malware', a shortened combination of the words malicious and software, is a catch-all term for any sort of software designed with malicious intent. That malicious intent is often theft of your private information or the creation of a 'backdoor' to your computer so someone can gain access to it without your permission. However, software that does anything it didn't tell you it was going to do could be considered malware.

Password protection

A security process that protects information accessible via computers that needs to be protected from certain users. Password protection allows only those with an authorised password to gain access to certain information.

Personal data

The General Data Protection Regulation (GDPR) defines personal data as any information relating to an identified or identifiable natural person ('data subject'); an identifiable natural person is one who can be identified, directly or indirectly, in particular by reference to an identifier such as a name, an identification number, location data or an online identifier – or to one or more factors specific to the physical, physiological, genetic, mental, economic, cultural or social identity of that natural person. The GDPR applies to personal data only if it is processed:

- wholly or partly by automated means (or is information in electronic form)
- in a non-automated manner that will form part of a 'filing system' (including written records in a manual filing system).

Phishing

A fraudulent practice in which private data is captured on websites or through an email designed to look like it is from a trusted third party. Typically, phishing scams involve an email alerting the user to a problem with their bank or another account.

Software

The part of the computer system that consists of data or computer instructions.

Spoofed Wi-Fi

A spoofed Wi-Fi will give you internet access while stealing the login information for any site you visit.

Synchronous communications

These are interactions between client and counsellor at the same point in time.

Text-based counselling

This is the use of 'text only' as the modality for counselling.

Text messaging

The act of composing and sending electronic messages – typically consisting of alphabetic and numeric characters – between two or more users of mobile phones, tablets, desktops/laptops or other devices. Text messages may be sent over a mobile network or via an internet connection.

Third-party services

A third party is an entity that is involved in some way in an interaction that is primarily between two other entities. The third party may or may not be officially a part of the transaction between the two primary entities, and may or may not be interacting transparently and/or legally.

Two-factor authentication

Two-Factor Authentication (2FA), often referred to as 'two-step verification', is a security process in which the user provides two authentication factors to verify they are who they say they are. For example, a service might ask for your password and then follow it up by asking you a security question (e.g. your mother's maiden name). Others will send a code to your telephone that you then input after entering your password. 2FA can be contrasted with single-factor authentication (SFA), a security process in which the user provides only one factor – typically a password.

Video-counselling

This is a synchronous counselling service where the client and counsellor communicate using a webcam, land line and encrypted internet software through which both parties are able to see and hear each other, and to share and create documents in real time.

Virtual private network

A virtual private network (VPN) is a technology that creates a safe and encrypted connection over a less secure network, such as the internet. VPN technology was developed as a way to allow remote users and branch offices to access corporate applications and other resources securely. To ensure safety, data travels through secure 'tunnels', and VPN users must use authentication methods – including passwords, tokens and other unique identification methods – to gain access to the VPN.

Technological competence

It is the responsibility of the counsellor to make sure that antivirus, encryption, pop-up blockers and other technological software tools are up-to-date and do not interfere with the therapeutic process. You need to be able to inform clients about what technology they need to work online, and warn them about common technological failures, such as Wi-Fi disconnecting or being of poor quality. Some clients may have broadband that does not support video-calling. You also need to inform clients of any potential security risks as part of the assessment procedure, particularly if the client may be affected by domestic abuse.

It's also important to ensure that you close down all other programs and apps before starting a video call, so that:

- automatic updates don't suddenly kick in and slow down your technology mid-call
- your device doesn't make rings, beeps or other sounds while you are engaged in online counselling.

Training source
The vendors of the technology you choose to use in your work will have training videos and a support service; these can help you learn how to use the app/program and find answers to any problems. You may well also find helpful videos on YouTube, but do start with the vendors' own material and support.

Don't forget that any such training can be recorded as continuing professional development (CPD), and counted towards your ethical body's annual requirements.

Speed-testing
Being able to offer video-counselling depends on your broadband speed; checking this in advance is essential. Bear in mind that:

- at peak times, speeds can slow down (such times might not be when you would expect – e.g. mid-afternoon can be problematic, with children returning from school)

- if multiple people are using your Wi-Fi router, speeds will slow down
- the client's broadband speed may be slower than yours.

Questions to reflect on
- How experienced are you in using technology?
- Does using technology hold any fears for you?
- How confident are you in explaining to a third party how a specific app, program or piece of technology works?
- Do you feel comfortable working online?
- Do you have the equipment, broadband connection and strength of mobile-phone signal to offer online counselling?

Task to complete
- Team up with your buddy or a colleague, and practise using the tools and technology, explaining to each other how to get started, and supporting each other in troubleshooting and resolving any technical hitches.

Clients' Relationship with Technology

It is not only your own equipment and relationship with technology that influences whether or not you can offer online therapy to a particular client.

Imagine that a client contacts you on the telephone for face-to-face therapy. They have been trying to find the courage to speak to someone for years. You make an appointment, and give them your address and postcode. They can drive but are not very good at using a satnav or reading a map. On the day of the appointment, they get in the car but – even with the best of directions – they can't find you. They ring you but – even with your help – they drive around in circles. Eventually, they give up and go home.

To translate this scenario into online working, owning a computer or even a smartphone does not mean that a client necessarily has the skill set or understanding to use it for online work. Asking general questions such as 'Do you use Skype or Zoom?' or 'How confident are you with technology?' will help you assess whether they have a sufficient level of skill and understanding to get them online.

Possible approaches
It can be useful to explore clients' fear or reticence at the idea of using technology; in doing so, it's important that you, as the therapist, come over as positive and confident, but are also congruent about any similar fear or reticence you may have experienced when the technology was new to you too.

If a client does not feel at all confident to work online, it may be that telephone counselling would be more suitable for them.

For all clients, it is a good idea to produce and send them a simple guide to the technology you have together chosen to use. I have included a example of a set of plain-English instructions about Zoom technology. This is not intended as a model, but more as a starting point for you to create your own guide. You are likely to need a separate guide for each type of technology that you will be using.

You can download this example from within the free online companion course by visiting counsellingtutor.com/online

How to Join a Zoom Meeting

NOTE: Before joining a Zoom meeting on a computer or mobile device, you can download the Zoom app from https://zoom.us/download. Otherwise, you will be prompted to download and install Zoom when you click a join link.

1. Click on the **Join Zoom Meeting** link.

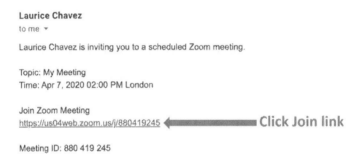

2. A new window will pop up. Click on the **Open Zoom.us** button.

3. Another pop-up will appear. Click on **Join with Computer Audio**.

4. You have now joined your Zoom meeting. You should be able to see/hear the other participant(s) in the meeting.

Managing the client's confidentiality

Helping the client understand how to protect themselves online can take many forms, such as:

- checking with them whether the room they are using is private, and that they cannot be overheard
- helping them understand that having lots of devices connected may slow their speed down
- making them aware of the risks when working online.

For any relationship to work, it needs to be reciprocal. You also need to feel comfortable and safe yourself. Some therapists may have had bad experiences with online dating or have been stalked through social media. It's worth remembering that countertransference can come from inanimate objects. If you don't feel comfortable with online work, it is essential that you speak with your supervisor.

Questions to reflect on
- What questions may be helpful to ask the client to assess their understanding of IT?
- What will you do if the client lacks confidence in using technology?
- How does the client feel about seeing themselves on screen?

Task to complete
- Create user guides for the platforms that you will be working on, which you will be able to send to your clients.

Presenting Online Counselling to Your Client

As you will already have seen, online work begins long before you have a formal session with a client. Before we can work therapeutically, your client needs to make an informed decision on whether or not online therapy will be a good fit for them.

It is likely that your client may not be fully informed as to what remote therapy is, how it works, and what the benefits and challenges may be for them. It is your duty to act in favour of a potential client's autonomy and give them the information they need to make an informed decision. Client autonomy is paramount in counselling – just as nobody should be 'sent' for counselling, nor should anyone be 'told' which technology will be used. Instead, they should be given the information they need to make a balanced decision for themselves. This is likely to lead to more effective therapy, and a greater client investment in it.

The process of informing your client starts at the first 'touchpoint', which may be your website or any place a client could discover your details (e.g. a listing in a counselling directory, a flyer placed in a clinic or a recommendation/referral by a third party). At each of these touchpoints, you need to begin outlining what you offer and how the potential client can find out more information.

Questions to reflect on
- What challenges do you think a client may need to overcome?
- What support do you need as a counsellor in moving to work online and/or by telephone?

Tasks to complete
- Reflect on the benefits and challenges that online therapy may hold for you (perhaps through journaling about this to explore your thoughts and feelings, and talking to others).

Suitability and Assessment

Working to professional standards is just as vital in online as it is in face-to-face therapy. The *Ethical Framework for the Counselling Professions* (BACP, 2018: 15) says:

> We will fulfil the ethical principles and values set out in this *Ethical Framework* regardless of whether working online, face-to-face or using any other methods of communication. The technical and practical knowledge may vary according to how services are delivered but all our services will be delivered to at least fundamental professional standards or better.

To do this, we must work within our competence. Assessment is a key part of doing our best to ensure – before we embark on counselling a client – that the client is a good fit for the modality and competence level of the practitioner. If they are not, then the responsible action is to make an appropriate and well-managed referral. For good reason, assessment happens before the therapeutic relationship begins. We undertake assessment to reduce the risk of having to interrupt the client's journey later in the relationship when the therapeutic relationship has been fully established.

Additional considerations in assessment for online therapy
All the usual areas that you would cover in assessing a client for face-to-face work also apply in assessment for online sessions, but there are some additional areas to think about, including the client's:

- preferences and competences in using the various forms of technology
- use of social media and existing online relationships and/or online groups
- attitude towards and suitability for online counselling
- access to a private, safe space in which to participate in online therapy
- psychological and physical difficulties that may affect use of technology, and any appropriate software support required
- ability to communicate emotions using the various technologies
- presenting issues.

Using measures

As a tool in assessing risk and thus suitability for online therapy, you may wish to use one or more mental-health questionnaires. These come in various forms, measuring depression (e.g. PHQ-9 and Beck's Depression Inventory), anxiety (e.g. GAD-7), stress (e.g. PSS) and overall mental wellbeing (e.g. CORE and WEMWBS). Many of these include questions that relate to suicidality (e.g. in PHQ-9, there is 'Thoughts that you would be better off dead or of hurting yourself in some way', assessing suicidal ideation; and in CORE-10, there is 'I made plans to end my life', assessing suicidal planning). There are then specific instruments available to measure suicidality – for example, the Beck Scale for Suicidal Ideation. These assess how far along the suicidal continuum the client currently is. Jones and Stokes (2009: 145) note: 'Evidence of serious risk in one of these categories may indicate that you would prefer to refer the client to other services (Samaritans, doctor etc.) or f2f counselling.'

Finding out what sort of communication the client prefers is essential in offering both choice and autonomy. In an ideal world, offering the choice of online or face-to-face sessions is preferable. Some clients may prefer to use the telephone because they have difficulty with their physical appearance or because of convenience. Other clients may prefer face-to-face work via a video-conferencing service, such as Zoom. There are various other key areas to investigate before beginning online therapy with clients. These are described in the paragraphs that follow.

How knowledgeable is the client about online counselling and relationships?

Finding out whether the client understands the nature of online counselling and of the client–counsellor relationship is essential. Some clients may see online counselling as social chitchat or an information/advice service. Assessing what the client expects from online therapy is much like assessing for face-to-face work, while also discussing issues such as disinhibition, the possibility of technological disruptions, data security, and the lack of nonverbal communication (for non-visual forms of online therapy).

Can the client read and respond to emails?

The very nature of online therapy demands that at some point you will communicate with clients via text or email. Therapists need to be sure that clients have the ability to read and understand written material, and can comprehend the content. This is particularly relevant when sending contracts or written instructions.

How might the client's presenting issues or diagnosis influence suitability?
Traditionally, online courses recommend caution when considering whether to work with the following client presentations:

- *Eating disorders* – unless you are an experienced therapist, you need to think carefully about working online with a client with an eating disorder. This is because it can be very hard to assess how the client is doing and – crucially – whether they are at risk.
- *Personality disorders* – there is a wide range of types of personality disorder and levels of severity. Practitioners must take care in the initial assessment to identify any areas of risk such as dissociative disorders, reactive attachment, paranoia, psychosis, self-harm and life-ending thinking. Consider how you would access external support for the client if they became unwell during the session.
- *Severe mental-health conditions* – if a client has a mental-health condition that leads them to experience psychosis, then it may not be possible to achieve psychological contact. Again, this can be accentuated in online working. You may be able to offer the person shorter 'holding' calls (rather engaging in full-on therapy) while you refer them to and they await – a more appropriate service. It's possible that experienced practitioners may be better able to assess their needs and so to use an approach themselves that would be helpful.

- *Risks such as self-harm, suicidal thinking or risky behaviours* – these can be challenging because we may not be able physically to see cut marks (for example on the client's arms), so we have to trust their reporting. This can lead to deeper trust, but can also lead to missed signs of risk. In online work, we therefore need to be more verbally explicit and direct, e.g. asking questions such as 'Have you self-harmed since we last spoke?' or 'Have you been thinking about killing yourself?'
- *Domestic violence* – this area needs lots of consideration regarding risk. Consider what would happen if the abuser found your details on the victim's mobile phone or overheard the victim speaking with you.
- *Addiction* – clients with addiction issues are often thought to be unsuitable for online therapy. It can be incredibly challenging because – as with self-harming behaviours – we are again relying on self-reporting, e.g. we can't smell alcohol, look closely at the client's pupils or do a drug test (if it's a treatment programme).

It is your responsibility as the therapist – with support, as appropriate, from your clinical supervisor – to think carefully about managing risk. It is also important – just as in face-to-face work – that your skill set is a suitable match for the client's issues and for what they wish to get from counselling.

Might the therapy be impacted by physical, medical or cultural factors?
If the potential client has any visual, auditory, speech, hearing loss or motor disabilities, has any serious medical condition, is

on medication or is receiving medical treatment in a hospital, you need to consider how these factors may affect their motivation and ability to use online therapy. It is also important to be vigilant for any signs that possibly indicate a medical condition that may need to be assessed in person by a doctor.

The online counsellor will likely receive requests for therapy by clients who have different cultural norms. Counsellors will have to assess whether they can communicate with and understand each other effectively. Some communities have a communal way of living and interacting; this could affect confidentiality. It is important to ensure that the client understands counselling to be a one-to-one activity.

Referral onwards
Your assessment of the client's suitability for online therapy may lead you to the conclusion that an onward referral or signposting is needed. As a counsellor, you will already understand how to handle this process in general, but a key difference from face-to-face working here is that the client may well live a long way from your area. As it may be difficult for you to have detailed knowledge of agencies in other localities, it can therefore be useful to focus instead on national services.

Questions to reflect on
- Do you need a written assessment policy, and list of questions to ask?
- What procedures do you need to put in place, and how?
- Do you have a solid referral pathway if counselling is not the service that the client requires?

Asynchronous versus Synchronous Communication

'Synchronous communication' can be defined as 'real-time communication between two people'. Examples include face-to-face, telephone or video-conferencing (e.g. Zoom) communication. This form of communication allows both parties to clarify misunderstandings in real time. Asynchronous communication, meanwhile, is when you send a message without expecting an immediate response – for example, using text, social media, email or online forums. This form of communication has to be 'interpreted' by the recipient. Because of the lack of real-time clarification, misunderstandings can arise more easily. Live-chat exchanges, meanwhile, fall between asynchronous and synchronous communication.

For example, you may be aware of the working relationship between Freud and Jung. What is not widely known is what contributed to the collapse of this. They corresponded through letters and – as time went on – their communication became more and more acrimonious. Is it possible that communicating by only this one medium contributed to the breakdown in their relationship?

Asynchronous communication

For counsellors who have so far been trained in and practised face-to-face working, asynchronous communication may feel rather alien – though even the email communication that you may use to set up synchronous sessions is of course asynchronous. Some counsellors may combine the two communication modes, for example having fortnightly face-to-face sessions, with therapeutic email exchanges between sessions.

Asynchronous communication may not suit all counsellors – for example, if you are dyslexic, text-based working may be both challenging and unpleasurable for you, and so would probably also not be in the best interests of the client.

You can see an example of an asynchronous (text-based by email) session below. This illustrates the difference in both dialogue and spontaneity between this method of communication and the more familiar synchronous communication. A commentary is provided on how the therapy is progressing, and the counsellor's rationale for the interventions.

 You can download this example from within the free online companion course by visiting counsellingtutor.com/online

Asynchronous Communication – Case Study

Client: *Jack, it feels a bit weird to me to be having my counselling online.*

This comment marks where this client is at the beginning. She feels the medium is strange, and is unsure of how it may work.

[A little later in the same exchange]

Client: *You hit the nail on the head there, when you said that I'm feeling conflict about this.*

The counsellor can identify the beginning of the relationship forming: the client feels understood and her feelings valued. The relationship has strengthened, resulting in this client feeling safe to bring real-life material that she has not felt comfortable sharing before. There is evidence of a sustained relationship using computer-mediated technology. Her next words substantiate this.

Client: *It's dawned on me through our exchanges that I tend to bottle up my feelings instead of talking openly about them. But somehow I can do that with you.*

The client needs to feel understood, heard and valued – and to feel that her issues are at the centre of the sessions. Prior to the below exchange, the client has expressed feelings but has said she felt they may be seen as silly. This is a high risk for the client, but the counsellor stays with her and maintains a client-centred focus.

Counsellor: *Gill, when I read your words, I do not for a moment think your feelings of sorrow, of unhappiness, of loneliness and your feelings of avoiding the*

	relationships and happiness you so desperately want are in any way silly or superficial.
Client:	*I'm so grateful for your words, Jack. It actually moved me to tears when I read it, which I never would have thought could happen for me, just from reading a message. I'd never seen myself as brave, and was worried I'd spoken out wrongly, but you've really understood and reassured me there.*

The client clearly feels empathy, feeling valued and understood. Her courage has been recognised, and this has resonated at a deep level, showing how important it is to maintain focus on the client, staying in their frame of reference. The counsellor next uses questioning to clarify, with respect for the client's frame of reference.

Counsellor:	*Almost watching others in relationships yet feeling not able to have what you so deeply want. Do I understand this correctly?*
Client:	*That sums it up well. I can't remember a time when I didn't envy all the people I know who have partners.*

The clarifying question deepens the relationship, and the client delves more deeply into the material, feeling understood and not judged. In the below example, a question was more directive and highlights the counsellor's misunderstanding.

Counsellor:	*So it sounds like you've always found men emotionally unavailable, Gill?*

Client: *No, I didn't mean it like that. I was trying to say it's especially hard for me to open up to men.*

The counsellor got this wrong – but, by him checking this with a question, the client is able to correct him. This demonstrates the importance of checking and clarifying when working online. Reflecting afterwards, the counsellor realises that he brought his own expectations and judgement into this relationship; he made assumptions based on experiences from his own life that did not match the client's frame of reference. This exchange left him feeling uneasy between sessions; he didn't know how the client was feeling in that time, as – without immediate feedback – there is no indication.

Counsellor: *I don't feel that it was you who didn't phrase this correctly, Gill. I feel this was me mixing my own emotions into your words.*

The counsellor is able to acknowledge his part and learn a valuable lesson of how long a week can seem when you feel something is out of place. This projection could have fractured the relationship. The client could have felt misunderstood and alone, and this could have affected the outcome. By acknowledging his projection and taking responsibility for it, the counsellor demonstrates congruence and shows that he is only human. In this case, it does not seem to have affected the relationship. With the gap between sessions being a week long, the counsellor uses summarising at the end of each exchange to feed back his understanding, and to open that up to the client for clarification and further exploration.

Counsellor: *In closing, I recognise the turmoil within you regarding letting anyone get emotionally close to you. I hear the pattern of breaking off relationships, even with people you really liked, to avoid making yourself vulnerable. I hear the conflict of getting to a place where you are feeling strong enough to take the next step, but then questioning whether the person is good for you, and the dilemma of asking yourself whether your feelings can be trusted.*

Client: *I really appreciate your response, Jack. As I'm writing now, it's like a fuzzy picture has suddenly come into focus. I can see the way ahead at long last.*

Feeling heard and having feelings summarised gives the client clarity, and the counsellor can see definite movement within the relationship. The counsellor found he used paraphrasing regularly to condense the feelings in each paragraph. He felt that when the client moved from one process to another, a paraphrase helped crystallise her feelings before moving on.

Counsellor: *You have reflected on how you feel, and trust your instincts are correct. You are recognising that just because you now feel ready to take a huge step, that does not mean you will take that step with just anybody. It seems like you have taken the control here, Gill. You are the one making the decisions on the direction of your life, and you decide who feels right for you.*

Client: *It is empowering to have taken control, but daunting too to know I have to start again looking for a partner.*

The counsellor's paraphrase led to a significant change in the client's life: she made a difficult decision that she felt was necessary for her happiness.

Client: *I'm aware as I'm writing that this is our last exchange, at least for now, and I feel like I'm going to miss therapy with you as I've really got a lot from it. But I know too that I'm able to move ahead more confidently now.*

The ending had been prepared for from the beginning (via the counselling contract), even before the first session started. The client's words here clearly show that this was anticipated by the client and – sad as endings can still be – was expected, planned for and in the client's control. The counsellor was careful not to dig deeply into any new material as he and the client approached their ending. To conclude, Jack summarised how he had experienced their relationship, and highlighted the privilege of being part of Gill's journey.

Beginning asynchronous communication

You may choose to use an automated reply when a client's enquiry comes in, in order to:

- let the potential client know that their message has been received

- tell them when they can expect to hear back from you
- offer emergency information if needed.

In your first proper message after this automated reply, you will:

- begin to build an online relationship
- clarify boundaries
- outline the structure on offer (including the length and number of sessions)
- invite the client to decide whether they wish to go ahead (so supporting client autonomy)
- provide the opportunity to ask any questions so they can clarify anything they feel unsure about.

Key skills in asynchronous communication
When responding to text-based communications, some good-practice tips are to:

- answer the client paragraph by paragraph, writing each of your responses underneath the relevant part of their communication
- focus on your empathy, working hard to put yourself in the client's frame of reference and understand their feelings
- reflect and paraphrase their feelings, rather than attempting to interpret these
- be brief and concise in your responses
- reread your response to check that you are happy with it and that it reads clearly before sending it, being especially vigilant for any ambiguity (so as to minimise the risk of being misunderstood).

Disinhibition Effect

When we study counselling, we learn about hidden psychological factors that can impact on how therapy is delivered and received. An example is transference, where a subconscious transaction can affect how the client sees the counsellor in the present moment. When transference goes undetected, there is a danger that the counsellor may begin acting from a position of countertransference rather than seeing and responding to the client in the 'here and now'. While we do not dive into the complexities of transference and countertransference here, we mention these concepts to illustrate how unseen psychological factors can infiltrate the therapeutic relationship and change its dynamics in such a way that therapy becomes less effective.

The disinhibition effect is a psychological factor that can manifest itself in a remote therapeutic relationship. Just as we had to study transference theory in order to work safely and effectively face-to-face, so we must understand the disinhibition effect in order to work ethically online.

The term 'disinhibition' refers to a lack of restraint or disregard of social conventions. If a person is disinhibited, they may act without forethought and without regard to risk. An example may be someone going on a night out, having a few too many drinks, and then finding themselves acting and behaving in ways that would normally be out of character for them. In the moment, disinhibition can feel liberating and even create a feeling of euphoria, but it can also carry a price tag of regret, guilt, remorse or shame when the behaviour is looked at retrospectively – and leave an emotional scar that lasts a lifetime.

The disinhibition effect can bring about these feelings in online clients: it's like the remoteness of the online world makes things feel less real. To use a simple example to illustrate the disinhibition effect, the online dating app Tinder shows pictures of possible people to date, and encourages a person to rate them as either attractive or unattractive by swiping left or right on a touchscreen. At the time of writing, there are 57 million people using Tinder worldwide, and 1.6 billon swipes are made daily: in other words, 1.6 billion decisions are made every single day based on perception of a person's attractiveness alone.

The feeling of 'distance' created by being online makes this judgement an easy, thoughtless process: it creates a kind of 'bravery' of being out of range. It's as if the people being judged are seen not as real human beings, but as pictures. But if those swiping online were asked to make the same judgement to a live person in a face-to-face situation, the psychology would change. It would be much more obvious that behind every picture is a real person, who experiences real emotions.

Online, it feels easier to leave negative comments; engage in bullying or trolling; make sexual advances; make judgements based on race, sexuality, culture or any other difference; or claim to be an expert in any given subject. There is a disconnect between online and real life that creates an environment where a person may act differently from how they would in a face-to-face setting. We must study and understand the disinhibition effect when considering working online as it is a reality that can affect the therapeutic relationship.

Background of the term 'disinhibition effect'
The term 'disinhibition effect' was first coined by psychologist John Suler in his 2004 paper 'The Online Disinhibition Effect'. Suler noticed that some clients self-disclose more readily and/or act out more often or more intensely online than they would face-to-face. This can lead the client to feel overwhelmed, foolish or anxious – or to fail to return for the next session at all. A similar phenomenon has also been observed in online dating.

He explored six factors that together can create this effect:

- dissociative anonymity ('You don't know me')
- invisibility ('You can't see me')

- asynchronicity ('See you later')
- solipsistic introjection ('It's all in my head')
- dissociative imagination ('It's just a game')
- minimisation of status and authority ('Your rules don't apply here').

Dissociative anonymity
One of the principal factors behind the online disinhibition effect is that you can use the internet with relative anonymity. It is not unusual for a client to feel protected and to experience reduced feelings of vulnerability. Online clients may disclose personal information very quickly, and so become overwhelmed.

Invisibility
When using text-based or online services, clients' inhibitions may become lower. Potential clients may misrepresent themselves, pretending to be someone they are not. While it is generally important to accept clients at face value, do bear in mind that, when working online, it is possible that your client is not who they say they are.

Asynchronicity
This is sometimes referred to as 'post and run'. In other words, when communicating by email or text, clients may 'do an online doorknob'. The asynchronous nature of email or text may lead clients to disclose information they would not have disclosed if they were working with you in real time. Disclosing via email or text may be cathartic for the client, allowing them to share information to avoid judgement or questions. Clients sometimes subvocalise as they write/read, leading to a perception that

they are talking to themselves. Talking to oneself can lead to disinhibition or oversharing.

If a client 'doorknobs' via email or text, be very thoughtful of how you address this. They may not realise how much they have shared. This may leave you considering whether you should raise the disclosure at the next session or wait for the client to bring it up.

Solipsistic introjection
One of the differences when working online as opposed to face-to-face is not 'seeing all' of each other: we may not see the person we are speaking to at all (e.g. when working by telephone) or we may see only their head and shoulders (e.g. when working on an online video platform). This can lead to either party assigning a persona or imagined characteristics to the other. Clients who use telephone or email counselling can be particularly susceptible to this; this can lead to professional boundaries being crossed.

We can help minimise the risk of solipsistic introjection by including a good-quality profile picture on our information, to remove the element of mystery about what we look like.

Dissociative imagination
Emily Finch, a lawyer who studies identity theft in cyberspace, observes that people might see cyberspace as a game in which the standard rules of everyday interaction do not apply. Clients may see online therapy as just a game to play out a fantasy, and this can happen with telephone counselling, where the client is a voice on the end of the telephone. Clients may become

disinhibited and cross boundaries; this can also occur with therapists!

Minimisation of status and authority

In the online world, status and authority are significantly reduced. Therapists may find that the power balance is very different online. The main area to consider here is that of boundaries, which can be breached when disinhibition kicks in.

Responding to the disinhibition effect

As therapists, we may need to control the speed of the client's disclosure, gently slowing this down while we build trust and the therapeutic relationship. Rapid disclosure may be fuelled by clients believing that getting it 'off their chest' will in itself make them feel better – yet in reality doing so might leave them with shame.

As therapists, we must also take care not to become more directive than we would usually be in our face-to-face work: doing so can be another product of the disinhibition effect.

However, supporting the client in applying grounding techniques may be helpful in online and telephone counselling as a way to ensure that the client doesn't move too fast for their own wellbeing. For example, we can encourage the client to contextualise their emotions, and to observe how their bodily sensations link with these. Grounding techniques can help clients to reconnect with their surroundings, bringing them out of a dreamlike state where things don't feel real.

In conclusion, the disinhibition effect makes it especially important to ensure that you have regular clinical supervision with a supervisor who is themselves experienced in online working.

Online Contracting

So you have already sent an initial contact response and agreement form (including information about online counselling) to your potential client. If they do decide to proceed, then what comes next?

Importance of Contracting
Just as in face-to-face work, a written contract is essential in the ethical practice of counselling. Contracts:

- give a clear indication on what is on offer
- specify the limits of confidentiality

- outline session times and duration of therapy
- state what fees are being charged
- summarise cancellation policies
- outline data-protection protocols.

The counselling contract must be written rather than verbal because:

- clients can then look over the contract and make a decision
- the counsellor is protected if a complaint is made against them
- it creates a professional impression of the service being offered.

Do remember that if a client makes a complaint, your ethical body will almost certainly ask to see your contract.

In short, contracts give the client an informed choice of whether or not to go ahead with therapy. Made between the counsellor and the client, the contract needs to take account of:

- the law, including on the limits of confidentiality and on data protection
- organisational policies (for counsellors working within an agency setting)
- your professional body's ethical framework.

For example, the BACP (2018: 17) states:

We will give careful consideration to how we reach agreement with clients and will contract with them about the terms on which our services will be provided. Attention will be given to:

a. reaching an agreement or contract that takes account of each client's expressed needs and choices so far as possible
b. communicating terms and conditions of the agreement or contract in ways easily understood by the client and appropriate to their context
c. stating clearly how a client's confidentiality and privacy will be protected and any circumstances in which confidential or private information will be communicated to others
d. providing the client with a record or easy access to a record of what has been agreed
e. keeping a record of what has been agreed and of any changes or clarifications when they occur …

It is best practice to keep the contract simple but comprehensive. An example is given below.

 You can download this example from within the free online companion course by visiting counsellingtutor.com/online

Sample Contract

The contract is between the counsellor and the counsellor.

Counsellor responsibilities
- To be available at the agreed time
- To start and end on time

- To offer a quiet, appropriate and undisturbed space
- To maintain safe, professional boundaries
- To regard all contact and information as confidential unless there is reasonable doubt concerning the actual safety of the client or others
- To encourage client autonomy
- To work within the [your ethical body] *Ethical Framework* (available upon request), including regular supervision
- To review the therapeutic work and relationship regularly
- In the unlikely event of the counsellor cancelling, to offer an alternative appointment as soon as possible

Client responsibilities
- To attend punctually
- To give a minimum of 48 hours' notice when cancelling/ changing an appointment (or the full fee becomes payable)
- To pay for one session in advance, then [insert amount] per session in full at each appointment
- To limit communication with the counsellor outside agreed counselling sessions to making, changing or cancelling an appointment unless by prior arrangement
- To be respectful towards the counsellor and the counsellor's property
- To agree to give permission to contact the GP if the counsellor has serious concerns about risk to the client's self or others
- To discuss with the counsellor when the time feels right to end therapy
- To let the counsellor know of any other actual or potential therapeutic relationship

Signed by client............................. Date........................

Signed by counsellor...................... Date........................

This contract is subject to regular review by the counsellor or the client.

What the counsellor offers

What is on offer is counselling of a person-centred nature. This means that you are empowered to discover solutions to issues in a supportive environment. As a counsellor, I offer you my honesty and respect while we explore issues you feel you would like to bring to counselling at the times that we have agreed.

Confidentiality

There are boundaries and limits to confidentiality in certain cases. Confidentiality may be broken if:

- I believe you or others to be in danger or at serious risk of being harmed
- I am required to do so by subpoena (court order)
- You imply involvement in or knowledge of an act of terrorism, money laundering, drugs trafficking or behaviours that may, in my opinion, lead to harm or neglect of children and/or vulnerable adults.

Supervision and confidentiality

I monitor my own practice by attending regular supervision and am committed to my own self-development. There are times where aspects of our sessions will be taken to supervision to monitor my practice; at no time will your name or any identifiable information be mentioned, and my supervisor is also committed to our contracted confidentiality.

Records of sessions

I keep notes relating to our sessions for five years or in the case of a child for seven years after they turn 18.

Notes are stored securely and destroyed after the time outlined above. Under the 2018 Data Protection Act, you have the right to access your notes.

Contacting you

If I need to contact you between sessions (e.g. in the unlikely event of having to rearrange an imminent appointment), where and how would you prefer I contact you?

....

If you don't attend on time, would you like me to contact you? If so, how?

....

Contacting me

You may call me on [insert phone number] or send an emall to [Insert emall address]. It is not possible to leave a voicemail on my phone, so if I am unable to answer, please email or send a text and I will get back to you as soon as I can.

> **Non-attendance**
>
> If you cancel within less than the 48 hours' notice agreed, or fail to attend an appointment, the full session fee will be charged.
>
> Where did you hear about my service?.......................................

Do ensure too that – if your client requires the help of an interpreter or a support worker – this is covered in the contract, bearing in mind your professional body's guidance on this (e.g. BACP, 2019b).

Informed Consent

For consent to be valid, it must be voluntary and informed, and the person consenting must have the capacity to make the decision (NHS, 2019).

Voluntary consent means that the decision whether or not to consent must be made by the client themselves, and must not be influenced by pressure from the counsellor, friends or family. Informed consent means that the client must be given full information on what the therapy involves. Having capacity means that the client must be capable of giving consent, which means they understand the information given to them, and are able to use it to make an informed decision.

It is vital to consider the client's capacity to consent, particularly in the case of:

- children and young people

- vulnerable adults
- clients who present as hesitant or under pressure from other people or agencies to engage with counselling.

Moreover, getting informed consent is not a one-off event. You must regularly consider the client's ongoing ability to understand and participate in therapy.

Consideration for contracting in online counselling
When starting to work online and/or by telephone, you need to consider how your existing (face-to-face) contract will need to be amended in order to cover this way of working. For example, additional points that you may wish to consider include:

- technical instructions and troubleshooting (if contact is lost)
- privacy (of where the counsellor and the client will be speaking from)
- online data footprint, including for emails
- additional risks to confidentiality when working online
- how you will handle any online disclosure of risk to self or others
- where you are based geographically and how you can be contacted
- legal and ethical considerations, including the GDPR and working within your geographical jurisdiction
- your training, supervision and insurance for online working
- your policy on clients recording sessions

- how you wish the client to indicate their agreement to the contract
- payment methods.

Electronic signatures

Gaining the client's electronic signature can be a good way to ensure that you have their explicit agreement to the contract. This has the benefits of creating an audit trail so the therapist can be sure it was the client who signed the contract, of the response being fast, and of the system being highly secure.

There are companies providing confidential online software that allows a client to sign a document via a computer, tablet or mobile phone. These include:

- Contractually
- DocuSign
- e-SignLive
- e-Sign+
- Nitro Cloud
- PandaDoc
- RightSignature
- Sertifi
- Signable
- SignNow
- SignRequest
- Zoho Sign.

Online payment tools

Just as you can't get a client's signature in person in online counselling, nor can the online client physically hand you payment for the session. There are a number of tools that can facilitate online payment, including:

- Braintree
- Handepay
- PayPal
- Sage Pay
- Shopify
- Square
- Stripe
- takepayments
- Worldpay.

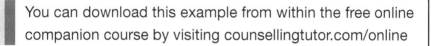
You can download this example from within the free online companion course by visiting counsellingtutor.com/online

Your Online Therapy Contract: Ethical Checklist

Have you included in your contract:

- welcome/introduction/inclusivity statement?
- confidentiality, including limitations, note storage, supervision and clinical will?
- cancellation policy fees, scheduling and payment instructions?
- legal and ethical considerations, e.g. liability and jurisdiction?
- membership of professional body and any other registrations (e.g. with the Information Commissioner's Office)?
- social media policy?

- technical instructions and troubleshooting, including the backup plan if the primary communication platform disconnects?
- guidelines for clients, e.g. creating a therapeutic space, smoking/drinking in sessions, and presence of companion animals?
- informed consent, including signatures?

Questions to reflect on
- Will all your clients be able to read written English?
- What will you do if the client does not return the contract?
- What would be the dangers of working without a contract in place?
- If you are charging a fee, how will you collect it online?

Task to complete
- Look over your existing (face-to-face) contract and amend it as needed to include the additional considerations needed for online working.

Using the Right Technology

One of the most common questions that is asked by counsellors who are preparing to enter online practice is: what technology should I be using? The answer is … (drumroll, please!) … that depends on you!

The main message here is that selecting the most appropriate technology for your practice is your responsibility. This will take research, as well as trial and error, as you try out different tools to discover which is the best fit for your practice.

Getting the right tools in place is likely to come at a cost. In the same way as you would need to invest in a room for face-to-face therapy, you will need to invest in the tools that will enable safe and confidential work online. You may be tempted to look for a solution in free tools – but beware that many free tools, such as social chat and video apps, do not offer adequate levels of confidentiality.

The phrase 'you get what you pay for' comes to mind here. If an application is free to use, there is a risk that it is monetised in a way that cannot be seen. An example is Facetime video; this is free to use, but Facebook collects data in order to target advertising at the user. If you took the time to read through the multiple pages of terms and conditions on some free social apps, you would be surprised at what data you are giving the company permission to collect and use. On some video applications, the terms and conditions cover how some calls may be recorded, listened to or intercepted so that the company can improve the service.

Deciding what technology is best for you means first deciding how you intend to work online. If you decide you are going to offer telephone counselling only, then a handset and SIM card may be all that is required. If you wish to offer text, email or video-counselling – or perhaps a choice of these – then you will need to find the tools to do the job.

Working via video
Working with video needs careful consideration. Lots of platforms advertise 'end-to-end' encryption, but just how

secure is it? A lot of people would be surprised to find out that the threat to confidentiality does not come from some evil hacker working in a darkened room surrounded by computers. Instead, it comes from the software companies themselves, whose employees can listen in (in order to monitor call quality) or collect data.

We cannot specifically recommend any particular tools for online working – you need to research these yourselves and make an informed decision. What is available, the related terms/conditions and the relevant law (e.g. on data protection) may change over time. Some tools are free of charge and others have an associated cost: again, you will need to weigh up the pros and cons of each tool before deciding what will best suit you and your clients.

At the time of writing, Zoom video-conferencing software is popular among private-practice therapists. It can have separate meeting rooms so that clients don't inadvertently come online and gate-crash another client's therapy. The software is free to download and use, and it has a simple interface that can be quickly learned: see https://zoom.us. VSee and Doxy.me are also widely used by online therapists: see https://vsee.com and https@//doxy.me/

Secure email
Another area that needs ethical attention is email. When communicating with a client, we have to consider how we ensure our email communication is secure enough to provide maximum confidentiality. Email accounts can be hacked or cloned; it is safer to use a web-based encrypted service, and to advise

clients not to consent to their web browser remembering their password. It is important that you use an email provider that is both secure and discrete. Hushmail is a popular choice for those working in online counselling: see https://www/hushmail.com/business/healthcare/hipaa-compliant-email/. Another possibility is Tutanota: https://tutanota.com/

The vendors of all the software and platforms mentioned here offer online training videos that can really help you get up and running. You may also like to refer to the following list of technological considerations for online working (CCPA, 2019: 13–15).

 You can download this example from within the free online companion course by visiting counsellingtutor.com/online

Technological Considerations for Online Working

General considerations

- Consider whether you and the client can be comfortable working without visual cues.
- Find sustainable ways to stay up-to-date with the trends and emerging research.
- Consider the privacy risks of the technology.
- Think about how the technology meets the client's clinical needs, including its likely impact on the therapeutic relationship. You may wish to search online for the evidence base for the technology in dealing with different client presentations.

Medium-specific considerations

Telephone

- Consider the security of your telephone connection.
- Take into account your and your client's location.
- Minimise or eliminate interruptions.
- Attend to tone and pitch of voice.
- Make more frequent vocalisations to indicate you are listening.
- After the call, securely delete the client's telephone number.
- If you work for an agency, use only agency telephones.
- Avoid using a personal mobile phone.

Email

- Have a secure and separate email address for clients.
- Use an encrypted system to communicate with clients, and password-protect any attachments.
- Work to compensate for the lack of visual cues, and to enhance the sense of experiencing the session in the moment.
- Pay attention to how much time you spend on a session.
- Remember that it takes skill to translate counselling into written words.

Text messaging

- Explore how your client views texting.
- Ensure you are using a secure text-messaging option.
- Be clear about what you will use text messaging for (e.g. to change appointments, to send reminders and to check in).
- Be clear about your likely response time to texts, so that not responding immediately is not misconstrued.

- Understand how emoticons and text abbreviations are used, including being familiar with the current slang in text messaging.

Live chat
- Bear in mind that this technology requires a different type of focus and patience.
- Consider your own and your client's typing speed.
- Close all other applications.
- Eliminate interruptions.

Video-conferencing
- Use a secure encrypted platform.
- Consider your bandwidth, lighting, background and clothing.
- Be mindful of the quality of your headset, reliability of sound/audio, and capability/compatibility of your and the client's devices.
- Check that the client has access to a private place where they cannot be overheard or interrupted.
- Consider and inform the client whether you will allow them to record sessions and, if so, how exactly they can use their recordings.

Questions to reflect on
- What CPD will you need around using technology?
- Will you practise using technology with a peer before meeting a client online?
- What support do you need?

Task to complete
- Research the tools you want to use for your online-counselling practice.

Chapter 2
Working Ethically and Legally Online

Ethical and Legal Requirements

Before beginning to counsel online, it is important to understand the additional ethical and legal requirements of using online technology to practise therapy, as opposed to working face-to-face.

The ethical body to which you belong will have its own code of ethics. While the BACP may not be your chosen body, we use this as our example here, since its *Ethical Framework for the Counselling Professions* (2018) is both robust and widely used by counsellors and psychotherapists.

If a client complains to your ethical body about you or the service that you provide online, it would expect you to be able to evidence justifiable decision-making, care and competence. You may be asked as a practitioner to evidence your competence to work online and your awareness of the additional ethical considerations.

Providing a service
Providing a service means you have an offer that is fit for purpose, and you can deliver what you promise. For example, you would not offer counselling in a room with broken windows, the door hanging off or chairs with broken legs! Clients will have a reasonable expectation that your service will meet their needs.

There are considerations such as undertaking training, making sure that the technology is fit for the purpose, and writing a set of online-specific policies and procedures.

The BACP's factsheet on working online in the counselling professions (2019a: 5) says: 'All practitioners should be sufficiently competent in the use of technology in their work to be able to provide reliable and adequate services to clients and colleagues.'

Competency with technology
You need to consider:

- providing an alternative form of communication if the primary method of communication fails
- keeping up-to-date with the technology being used
- understanding the security implications of technology with regard to confidentiality
- having technological support systems in place (i.e. planning who will fix it, if it goes wrong)
- being competent to deliver online services.

You may wish to consider taking a course on basic computer skills if you feel you need to polish these. Again, you can count this towards your annual CPD requirement for your ethical body.

Do be patient with yourself: it takes time to learn how to use new technology. As mentioned earlier, there are likely to be video tutorials on YouTube that can help you. Try out a few until you find one that fits your needs and learning style.

Security and confidentiality
When working online, do make sure that:

- you are up-to-date with the latest threats to security
- your virus protection is regularly updated
- anyone else accessing your technology does not have access to client information, such as chat logs, telephone numbers or text messages
- you are aware of data-protection issues or potential breaches in security
- you have read the 'small print' (terms and conditions) relating to client-facing software that you are using
- you remain vigilant to the risk of being overheard
- you have a password protecting your device to prevent 'physical intrusions'
- Wi-Fi points are secure and encrypted
- you remember that your device is only as secure as its last update
- you read any updates as software vendors change their terms of service
- you bear in mind that no system of electronic communication is 100% secure.

If things go wrong
Being honest and open in dealing with clients is both morally and ethically expected for therapists. Should a data breach occur, the BACP suggests:

- taking immediate action to prevent or limit any harm
- repairing any harm caused, as far as possible
- offering an apology, when this is appropriate

- notifying your supervisor and/or manager, and discussing what has occurred
- investigating and taking action to avoid whatever has gone wrong being repeated
- contacting the relevant authorities in your country about the breach, if indicated – e.g. in the case of a data-protection breach in the UK, you would need to inform the Information Commissioner's Office (ICO).

Being congruent about any breaches is important, helping to preserve the core conditions and showing the client that you are human and willing to own your errors.

Legal considerations
The main area of legality in online counselling is data protection. Most countries have legal protocols around the storage and sharing of data. In the UK, the Data Protection Act 2018 (the UK's implementation of the GDPR) covers areas such as:

- data storage
- data sharing
- what you should do in the case of a data breach
- policies and procedures you will need to follow in the event of a data breach.

Supervision and training
It's also essential that you practise what you preach! The old adage that the client can go only as far as the counsellor is willing to go is very true in the online-counselling world: so do

try to have supervision using the same medium (i.e. online or by telephone) that you are using to counsel clients. This can help give you a better sense of what the client experiences.

> *Questions to reflect on*
> - What policies and procedures will you have to put in place for online counselling?
> - What is your understanding of online security?
> - What is your understanding of data-protection law and procedure?
> - How do you feel about online supervision?

> *Task to complete*
> - Familiarise yourself with your device(s), using self-directed study as needed.

Best Fit for the Client

Online therapy may not be the best fit for clients, for various reasons.

Credibility

When thinking about offering an online service, one of the most significant factors is managing client expectations. While you may feel confident about working online, some clients may feel uncomfortable and think it is 'second-best'. Clients may also be concerned about their confidentiality and the ability to engage online or with technology. Some clients may feel that their issues are 'too big' for online therapy.

Lack of nonverbal cues
Like therapists, some clients may struggle with nonverbal cues. This is especially relevant in telephone counselling, though can also be true for online work as the quality of the image may not be perfect (e.g. due to internet connection, lighting, or seating position in relation to the camera). They may wonder how the therapist is reacting to what they are saying, or feel inhibited. It can be helpful to be more explicit about your body language, verbalising any such reactions.

Clients who use hearing aids or have limited hearing may also find the telephone difficult as they may be reliant on lip-reading.

Therapist's skill set
Therapists should also be thoughtful of their skill set when initially working with clients. Transferring face-to-face counselling skills into an online environment takes adaptation and practice. Consideration should be given to what sort of presenting issues you can work with – given your developing skill set.

Client presentation
As noted in 'Suitability and Assessment', clients presenting with eating disorders, personality disorders, severe mental-health conditions, risky behaviours (e.g. self-harm and suicidal thinking), domestic violence or addiction may not be appropriate for online work.

If online counselling is not a good fit for the client, you need to be prepared to signpost or refer them on to a suitable service that can provide the support they need. We look at this in more detail in Chapter 3.

Contact information

Key to safe and ethical working online is the collection of emergency contact details for each client (including their GP practice) before beginning therapy. Ensure that you then always have the relevant details on hand during every session in case you need to contact the emergency services (for risk of harm, falling over, having a seizure etc.). This is especially useful if you are working with a client abroad.

Questions to reflect on
- How do you assess your own competence?
- What procedure do you need for clients with presentations that are not a good fit for online therapy?
- What client information do you need to get from the client?

Task to complete
- Audit your skillset, considering what kind of presentations would and would not be a good fit for you.

Working within Your Jurisdiction

Working online via video link or by telephone has one very distinct difference from working face-to-face: your client can be anywhere. This way of working might seem at first sight to enable you to work with clients anywhere in the world – but in fact working across borders and internationally has implications that you need to consider before getting involved in doing so. There are additional challenges of working with a client in another country, and you may well need specific policies in place to do so ethically.

Legal aspects

It may be tempting to work with someone in a different country; however, the legal and ethical consequences could be very damaging. Different countries have different laws and qualification levels. In the USA, for instance, for the most part, therapists can work only within their state border. The reason for this is that each state has its unique licensing regulations. Therapists who contravene these restrictions can find themselves answering to their ethical body and may be subject to litigation; it may even be considered a criminal offence.

Moreover, your insurance company may not cover you in the event of a civil action if you work outside your jurisdiction.

Good practice

If you are considering working outside your jurisdiction:

- always ask the client where they are situated
- make yourself aware of the laws and ethical protocols of your client's country
- be aware that in some countries, the terms 'counsellor' and 'psychotherapist' are protected titles, and so using them could lead to prosecution for misrepresentation
- make sure that the client sends you their name and address – if the client moves to a different jurisdiction and fails to tell you, you can then evidence where the client was living when therapy began.

It can be helpful to state in your contract that the work is being undertaken under the laws and ethical guidelines of your own country. The BACP (2019a: 11) states:

One way of reducing the uncertainty is to explicitly state in the contract that the work is being undertaken in accordance with the laws of the practitioner's own country and any disputes will be subject to that country's law. This reduces the degree of uncertainty but does not eliminate it all together. Any contractual disputes would usually be considered in the legal system that applies to the practitioner, provided that this has been included in the contract between practitioner and client. However, any allegations of civil wrongs or crime by the practitioner could still be considered in the legal system that applies to the client's location.

Other considerations

If the client is in a different country, think about the following issues too:

- Who will you refer the client to if you can't meet their needs?
- Who will you contact if your client is at risk?
- Will you be able to communicate clearly with other agencies (e.g. if you don't speak their language)?
- Will your usual payment method work in the other country?

In short, it may well be best to work only within your own jurisdiction – and if you do decide to work beyond this, proceed with caution and only after you have thought through all the possible implications.

Insurance Considerations

Ensuring that you have in place appropriate insurance is of course vital, given that it is a requirement of ethical bodies. For example, the BACP's *Ethical Framework for the Counselling Professions* (2018: 15) states: 'We will be covered by adequate insurance when providing services directly or indirectly to the public.'

You can't assume that your insurance will necessarily cover you for online working, and in all territories. The BACP's factsheet on working online in the counselling professions (2019a: 12) says:

> Insurance policies for professional liability vary in whether they cover online or digital working with

clients or restrict online work to particular countries. Like any form of insurance, it is important for practitioners to make sure that they have the right type of insurance for the service being provided. If in doubt, ask your insurer.

If a client makes a complaint about your service, your insurance company will provide a legal representative to accompany you to any hearing. In the case of a civil action, your insurance policy will provide legal assistance and may pay out if the action is proved and compensation awarded. But insurance companies pay out only if you have abided by the terms and conditions of the policy. Being insured protects you only against the insured risks!

Actions needed
Before engaging in any online counselling, contact your insurance company outlining:

- exactly what you plan to offer in your practice
- what equipment you are using
- from which jurisdiction(s) you intend to accept clients
- whether or not you will be working with children or vulnerable adults
- whether you are working independently or for an organisation (e.g. a school, health service or charity)
- the relevant training you have received, including whether you are a qualified or a trainee counsellor.

Remember: if you do not give your insurance company the full facts, they may not cover you if you make a claim.

It is wise to contact the company by email rather than telephone, so that you have written evidence of their response; store this – along with your policy documents – in your secure filing system, so that you will always know where to find it. When you come to renew your insurance each year, do check again – just in case any changes have been made that you are not aware of.

Insurance types
There are two forms of insurance that therapists need to consider:

- public liability – this insurance pays out if a client is injured while on your premises (for example, if they trip over and break their arm)
- professional indemnity – this insurance pays out if a client brings a successful claim for malpractice.

Most organisations will have both these categories of insurance. However, if you work for an organisation, you should not rely on it to cover you fully. Insurance has to be activated by the person who pays the premiums. There have been cases where the organisation has declined to activate the insurance and left the therapist without cover. It's always wise therefore to buy your own cover: wherever you are working, it is *your* practice.

Questions to reflect on
- What insurance do you already have in place, and what extra might you need?
- When do you need this to take effect?

Online Confidentiality

There are additional considerations to consider when working online.

Client's confidentiality

When you contract with a client, make sure that you enquire whether their environment is confidential. Ask them whether they can be overheard or observed by anyone in the household. Sometimes, clients may not realise that their therapy session may be listened to by someone in the next room. It may be helpful for them to use a headset. If working with video, enquire how they feel about you being able to see into their home.

It's important to think not only about what medium you will use to conduct full sessions but also how you and the client will contact each other for any administrative matters (e.g. rearranging or cancelling a session). Email, telephone or text are generally preferable as they have the best likelihood of being secure – but do check with the client during contracting, and record their answers in writing – this way, you know and have a record of their contact consents. Don't be tempted to contact clients via private message to their social-media accounts: you never know who may intercept your message.

Therapist's confidentiality

Consider the possibility of accidental self-disclosure – in other words, if you will be working on a webcam from home, consider what the client will see in the background. For example, clients who are having counselling for fertility issues may find it difficult to be faced with pictures of their counsellor's children in the background. Some software (e.g. Zoom) allows you to use a photograph as a background; this can help preserve your privacy and can also provide the client with some stability in terms of the context in which they see you. For example, some therapists use a picture of their therapy room, which they can then apply when working from any other location. However, do test out the appearance of this first with a friend or relative, as sometimes the digital background can overlap the real therapist, and make you appear an unusual shape or even to be missing body parts.

Therapists also need to be thoughtful about their online presence. Some clients may do an online search for their therapist in the hope of finding out more about them. Any information found could lead to an uncomfortable discussion as the client wants to know more or asks direct questions. Checking your security settings on social media is an essential task for all counsellors, whether working face-to-face or online, so that clients can't access personal photos and posts that you may have uploaded, been tagged in or commented on. It can also be a good idea to change your name on social media – for example, some therapists choose to use their given name(s) and omit their family name, to abbreviate part or all of their name to initials, or to use a pseudonym.

Clinical wills

It's crucial that when we look at confidentiality, we consider every aspect. When people die, there is usually a need to administer the estate of the deceased. Therapists need to consider what would happen to their clients if they themselves became ill or incapacitated. Having a clinical will means that another professional can contact clients, offering support during the transition to another therapist.

In addition to the usual information that you might expect to include in a clinical will, online working will require you to add in other details, such as the passwords to your computer and other devices, and instructions on how to access your voice mail.

It is good practice to inform clients during contracting of what happens and who would contact them in case of your death or incapacity.

A possible template is included below, though we recommend that you take relevant legal or professional advice when considering this element of your practice.

You can download this example from within the free online companion course by visiting counsellingtutor.com/online

Template for Clinical Will When Working Online

I   ………………..

of (address) ………………..

                   ………………..

....

declare this to be my professional will.

It contains detailed instructions on how to manage my practice if I become unable to do so myself through injury, death or any other form of incapacitation.

I acknowledge that this is not a legal document. It provides detailed instructions on how to manage my practice, and offer continuing support and care to my clients, in the event of my death or incapacitation.

My ethical body: ....

My ethical body membership number: ....

My insurer: ....

My insurance policy number: ....

Password to my device(s): ....

How to access my voice mail: ....

Where my practice records are stored: ....

My supervisor's name and contact details: ....

My executor's name and contact details: ....

I hereby grant my executor the authority to act on my behalf.

My instructions are:
- to contact clients past and present
- to offer current clients a choice of referral options
- to notify relevant organisations or professional parties
- to store client notes and information appropriately

- to forward notes and details to any new counsellor the client may choose to work with (with the client's express permission)
- to close the practice both practically and financially.

Signed

Therapist: ………………..

Date: ………………..

Witness: ………………..

Date: ………………..

Questions to reflect on
- How will you approach the subject of the client's own confidentiality?
- How will you ensure that personal information is secure from searches being seen from my camera?
- How do you feel about writing a clinical will?

Tasks to complete
- Look at the space you will be working in and consider your background.
- Think about your clients' confidentiality and the considerations they need to make for their own confidentiality.
- Go through your contract again and adjust as needed for online confidentiality.
- Research clinical wills, and draft or review your own (using the template above if you wish), seeking legal or professional advice as appropriate.

Data Protection

Another aspect of working ethically and legally is ensuring that your systems properly protect clients' personal data. Data-protection regulations can be quite complex, and include legally binding aspects to which you must adhere in your practice. This legislation varies between countries. Here, we look at the law that applies to England, Wales, Northern Ireland, Scotland and countries within the European Union. It is your responsibility as a practitioner to research – and ensure you comply with – the laws covering data protection in your own geographical location.

At the time of writing, the GDPR has been in force for only a couple of years or so. This means that there has not been time yet for the building of a body of case law (i.e. how the law is practically interpreted and ruled on in court, as signalled by the outcomes of past cases). Thus, we will gain greater clarity on the GDPR and its requirements in counselling practice as time goes on.

Your obligations
In 2016, the GDPR was passed in the European parliament; in 2018, it became enforceable. GDPR legislation was a result of countries realising that existing data-protection legislation was inadequate in the face of internet growth and the exploitation of citizens' personal data. The GDPR covers the storage, distribution and security of personal data.

The GDPR distinguishes between 'data controllers' and 'data processors', defining each as follows:

- 'Controller' means the natural or legal person, public authority, agency or other body which, alone or jointly with others, determines the purposes and means of the processing of personal data.
- 'Processor' means a natural or legal person, public authority, agency or other body which processes personal data on behalf of the controller.

While data controllers are responsible for ensuring full compliance with the GDPR, data processors, you have more limited compliance responsibilities. If you store any client information on a personal device (such as a smartphone or computer – or even in a paper notebook), you are a data controller and are legally obliged to register with the ICO. This is likely to be true of private practitioners (Membrey and Mitchels, 2019). Meanwhile, counsellors working within an agency setting (including students) will usually be data processors, and so are not required to register with the ICO.

Age Appropriate Design Code
If you work with children and young people, do ensure that you are familiar with the Age Appropriate Design Code (ICO, 2020); this came into force in the UK on 2 September 2020, with a 12-month transition period, after which organisations will be expected to comply with it. The code may be extended to other countries in due course – so do check with the relevant authority in your country of practice. The Age Appropriate Design Code presents guidance on how to design websites and apps that are aimed at children and young people.

How long can I keep data for?
Generally speaking, clients can ask for their information to

be erased. There are some exceptions to this – medical and police records, for example. Therapists need to contact both their insurance company and ethical body to enquire how long they need to keep records. Time limits for storage of records must be stated and agreed in the contract before therapy takes place.

Clients' rights

Under the GDPR, clients have the right to access their notes or treatment plans. This can include chat logs, text messages or emails in which they are personally identifiable. This is done by the client submitting a subject access request either in writing or verbally. Organisations or individuals have 30 days to comply with the request.

Contracting

In your contract, you can state that the work is being undertaken under the laws and ethical guidelines of your (the practitioner's) own country. The BACP (2019a: 11) states: 'This reduces the degree of uncertainty but does not eliminate it all together. Any contractual disputes would usually be considered in the legal system that applies to the practitioner, provided that this has been included in the contract between practitioner and client.'

Using a privacy policy

A privacy policy is a statement that discloses how you gather, use, disclose and manage clients' data. It can help your clients to trust you and your business, and can help prevent problems and complaints – and protect you if this does happen.

Here is a sample privacy policy that you can adapt to your own practice by filling in the text in the square brackets as appropriate.

 You can download this example from within the free online companion course by visiting counsellingtutor.com/online

Privacy Policy

[Therapist's name] is committed to complying with the terms of the General Data Protection Regulation (GDPR), and to the responsible and secure use of your data. [Therapist's name] has a legitimate interest in processing personal data to provide counselling services.

The purpose of this statement is to let you know what personal information I collect and hold, why, how long it is stored for, and your rights over your personal data. I am registered with the Information Commissioner's Office (ICO), reference [registration number].

1. Information about you
- I collect personal information from you when you enquire about my counselling services and set up an initial appointment.
- This information includes contact details, your availability and other relevant personal information.
- Once you finish counselling, all data regarding your counselling is stored securely for seven [or change to fit

your insurance provider's requirements] years and then destroyed.

- When you enquire about counselling, I ask only for the contact details and personal information I need to answer your enquiries and to keep you informed.

2. My use of this information

- Your data will be used only to provide you with my services and to give you information relating to these.
- I will not share your details with any other person or organisation without your knowledge and permission unless there is a legal requirement as stated in the counselling contract or [any exceptions you may have].
- A breach of confidentiality is when someone shares information with another in circumstances where it is reasonable to expect that the information will be kept confidential.

3. Security

- I will take all reasonable precautions to prevent the loss, misuse or alteration of information you give me.
- Communications in connection with this service may be sent by email.
- For ease of use and compatibility, communications will not be sent in an encrypted form unless you require it and give me permission to communicate with you in that way.
- Email, unless encrypted, is not a fully secure means of communication.

- Whilst I endeavour to keep my systems and communications protected against viruses and other harmful effects, I cannot bear responsibility for all communications being virus-free.

4. Your rights over your personal data

- If you would like to see the information I hold about you, or would like to correct, update or delete any records, please email me at [therapist's email address].
- If you have any concerns about my use of your data, please contact me directly at [therapist's email address].
- I will do my utmost to resolve any concerns you have.
- If – for any reason – I cannot resolve your concerns, you may choose to contact the ICO directly.

Good practice

For all devices and systems on which you store client data, ask yourself the following questions:

- Are they secure (password-protected)?
- Are the virus and firewall software up-to-date and enabled?
- If the device was lost or stolen, could you delete the data remotely?
- Are client notes stored securely?
- When you change or sell your technology, how can you permanently delete data?

We include below a useful checklist on data-protection measures (CCPA, 2019).

Data-Protection Measures

Basic security measures

- Ensure you have up-to-date antivirus and anti-malware software.
- Ensure your browsers and operating systems are up-to-date.
- Enable disk encryption.
- Encrypt portable storage devices (e.g. USB sticks).
- Password-protect all your devices with strong passwords, using a different password for every website or app, and changing these every three months. You might like to use a password manager to help you with this, e.g. LastPass, Dashlane, 1Password or KeePass: https://www.which.co.uk/news/2018/11/stay-safe-shopping-online-with-the-best-password-managers/
- Produce a risk-management strategy that identifies your assets (both physical devices and data), the possible threats to these (e.g. theft or loss), the potential impact if this occurs, and what you will do to prevent or (in the worst case) respond to this. You may wish to document this as part of your security policy.

Wi-Fi security

- If you use Wi-Fi at your place of work, ensure it is secured.
- Do not use public Wi-Fi for sensitive information, because doing so is not secure, even when password-protected.

- Consider using your own mobile data in public places.
- Use a VPN (which is designed to provide a secure, encrypted 'tunnel' in which to transmit data).
- Watch out for 'spoofed' Wi-Fi. Fraudsters may set up a Wi-Fi hotspot of their own and disguise it as genuine public Wi-Fi. The spoofed connection has a name similar to the place where you are, e.g. a coffee shop, and allows you to browse as normal, but sends you to a fake website in an attempt to steal information from you. When using a public hotspot, ask a staff member for the full network name and make sure it matches exactly the one you connect to on your device. If you think a spoofed Wi-Fi connection is operating, tell the manager of the outlet you are in.
- Make sure your home Wi-Fi is secure, and do not allow guests to use it. If you have multiple computers on your Wi-Fi network, and you enable file-sharing on those computers, letting someone onto your network potentially exposes the data in those folders. You can set up a separate Wi-Fi network for guests.

Phishing protection

- If you receive an email that has an attachment in it and there is a request for you to open the attachment, look to see whether the email address actually matches the person it says it is from (by clicking on the name and looking at the email address).
- If you are at all suspicious, do not open or download the file. Contact the person and ask them if they sent you something.
- Banks don't send attachments, and businesses don't send invoices out of the blue. Always take a moment and

think about what you are looking at. Did you recently order something from this business?

- Links in phishing emails will often look like they are from 'yourbank.com/login', but the link will take you to another website. Always check the URL of the site you are on after you follow the link.
- If you are unsure whether or not an email is safe, assume it is unsafe. Do not click on the link. Contact the institution and ask them whether they are sending out emails.
- Companies in the UK and around the globe know about phishing. They do not send out emails asking you to provide your login information. Your company, agency or institution will not send you an email asking for your login and password information. If you receive an email like this, you should not trust it.

Hardware end of life

- Hardware, when it is no longer being used, has a lot of information on it. Simply recycling computers and tablets is not an option when they contain sensitive information.
- If your hardware is functioning when you decide to dispose of it, you should remove the hard drive.
- Deleting files does not remove them from a hard drive.
- Overwriting files is effective for preventing only some hackers from accessing the files.
- Even reformatting a drive doesn't completely remove information if the hacker is skilled enough.
- Store all information from your mobile phone onto the SIM (subscriber identification module) card before recycling

the phone. Then – unless you are transferring the card to a new phone – destroy the card.

Physical security of mobile devices

- Physically lock away your devices when not in use.
- Password-protect all devices and do not share those passwords with anyone.
- Never leave your devices unattended.
- Keep minimal client data on your devices (e.g. if a client texts you, securely delete the message as soon as you have read it).
- Have a data removal app so that if your device is stolen, you can wipe the data.
- For iPhone, enable *Find my iPhone*, which is an iCloud service. You can remotely lock your device and wipe your device. This works with all Apple devices.
- If you have a printout of passwords, keep it locked away.
- If you need to print out any client data (e.g. contact information in case of emergency), keep it locked away.

Software terms of use

- Read the fine print. Updates require you to agree to new terms and conditions as part of the updating process.
- Always reread the fine print if the company changes hands.
- Check all privacy policies for anything you are considering using (because you cannot promise any more than they can).
- Examine the backup policy, including whether data ever gets deleted and – if so – on what schedule, ensuring that this fits with any laws or regulations in your jurisdiction or

organisation that require certain types of records to be retained for specific periods of time.

- Determine whether the backup is encrypted; if so, who can decrypt the data? 'Zero-Knowledge' systems cannot decrypt your data (which helps ensure confidentiality) but also require you to take extra care not to lose the password.
- Know your system! Many services offer automatic backup of everything on your computer/mobile device (e.g. iCloud and Dropbox). Make sure that counselling records are not automatically backed up to a non-involved third party.
- Check the location of servers: records should be stored within the UK (or your own country of jurisdiction).
- Ensure you are aware of any specific agency and institution requirements.
- Check that the software provider allows you to use its product for commercial use.

Questions to reflect on
- Do I need to register with the ICO?
- Do I need to review what information I store, and how?
- What steps do I need to take to protect clients' data?
- What do I need to put in my contract about the GDPR?

Tasks to complete
- Look at and familiarise yourself with the data-protection rules that are in force for the country you are in.
- Audit the devices and systems on which you store client data.
- Write your own privacy policy, using the template provided above if you wish.

Your Disclaimer if Things Go Wrong

No matter how careful you are yourself to protect clients' personal data, things can still go wrong through no fault of your own. When you work online through any technological medium, you (and your clients) need to embrace an uncomfortable truth: technology is fallible and is not solely in your control; and there is a possibility (albeit a minimal one) that confidentiality may be compromised.

For this reason, it is really important that clients understand the limitations of technology regarding confidentiality. You can help manage clients' expectations by designing and using a disclaimer statement, to protect yourself from third-party error (i.e. by the providers of the technology you are using), such as data hacking.

Client autonomy

When thinking about your online practice, you must give the same weight to the client's decision-making as you would in face-to-face work. Making clients aware of the pitfalls of connecting using technology is an essential ethical principle. When the client is fully aware, they can make an informed decision, thus preserving client autonomy.

Your responsibilities

Writing a disclaimer does not protect you from blame if you misuse the technology or are negligent in breaching confidentiality. In other words, you need to understand the technology you are using and to keep abreast of any updates. First, you must ensure you read the 'small print' of your technology providers; the part of this that describes compliance with the GDPR is called the 'data processing agreement'.

It is good practice to sign up to your technology company's website or join their forums so that you keep up-to-date with any changes they implement and the impact these may have on confidentiality.

The real chances of a confidentiality breach due to the technology are probably very small, but – while we can always hope for the best – prudence requires us to plan for the worst.

You might find the following checklist helpful when weighing up whether you have considered all your responsibilities in working online.

 You can download this example from within the free online companion course by visiting counsellingtutor.com/online

Checklist for Online Working

Technology
- Are you satisfied that the video software you are using is secure?
- Are you confident that your computer/device is running the latest updates?
- Does your computer have a reliable malware/virus detector?
- Are you using a secure email address?

Telephone counselling
- Have you decided whether you need a separate mobile phone or phone number for counselling?
- Are all your devices (e.g. phones and computers) password-protected?

- Can you erase information off your phone/device if it is lost or stolen?

Assessment
- Have you assessed whether the client is suitable for counselling?
- Are the client's issues a good fit for your modality of therapy?
- Do you need – and have you performed – a risk assessment?
- Have you noted down the client's emergency contact details?
- Have you sent the client any measure questionnaires to fill in (e.g. CORE-10/34, PHQ-9 and GAD-7)?

Legal and ethical
- Have you informed your insurance company that you are working online?
- Are you working within your jurisdiction?
- Have you completed your living will?
- If the client is under 18, do you need to reference Gillick competence?
- Do you need a data processing agreement for the video software you are using?

Contractual
- Have you sent the client the disclaimer and received it back signed?
- Have you sent the client the contract and received it back signed?
- Have you sent the client a copy of the privacy policy?
- Do you need a therapy contract?

Questions to reflect on

- What do I need to put in my disclaimer (e.g. specifying which technology you use, and its compliance with the GDPR)?
- What forums or newsletters do I need to sign up to?
- What CPD do I need to complete to assure myself that I am competent with the technology I use?

Task to complete

- Prepare your disclaimer and look into the terms of third-party software providers, checking their GDPR compliance.

Chapter 3

Managing Risk Online

Referrals

All counsellors – whether working online or face-to-face – should have a referral strategy. There are several reasons why a practitioner may refer a client to another service or practitioner:

- The therapist's skill set or training is not a good fit for the client's presenting issues.
- The client needs support between sessions.
- The sessions offered may be insufficient for the client's presenting issues (e.g. in agencies that offer only short-term therapy).

It is a good idea to prepare the client for this eventuality by mentioning the concept of referral during contracting, explaining that this can sometimes be necessary and why. In particular, do ensure that you make clear to clients:

- what support they can reasonably expect to be provided by your service directly
- how you will seek any additional support required on their behalf
- what support they are responsible for seeking themselves.

Online resources or guidance may be provided to assist clients in finding appropriate emergency services, especially where clients are communicating from a distance, or where it is inappropriate or impractical for the practitioner to seek additional services on behalf of their clients.

Specific considerations in online counselling
When working online – and particularly by telephone, where visual contact is absent altogether – it is less obvious whether or not the client is who they say they are. It is not impossible that someone may impersonate another, for example in a bid to obtain confidential information. It is necessary therefore to take reasonable steps to check this, especially when working with children and young people, also confirming their age. This is important for child-protection purposes.

When working online, there are specific processes that you need to consider with regard to referrals. The first is that, unlike face-to-face work, your client is not in the same room; this means that negotiating a referral may mean that you are referring out of your local area. Second, managing risk is more complex, because the client is not physically present in your therapy room. This is particularly relevant for clients who:

- are drug users
- have eating disorders, especially those with an interest in websites that promote anorexia (known as 'pro-ana' sites)
- have severe mental-health issues
- self-harm, especially those who may be accessing online resources supporting this
- are at risk of taking their own life.

Assessing your skill set

Even the most competent and well-trained therapist may find themselves in difficulty when working online. Most counselling training focuses on face-to-face work and the ability to interpret your client's frame of reference in a holistic way. Denied the ability to see 'all' of the client, and relying on just what they say (certainly in telephone counselling), even the most experienced therapist may feel deskilled.

Identifying referral pathways

Having a list of national support networks (e.g. the Samaritans and Big White Wall) is a useful starting point. The advantage of using national agencies is that they are not region-specific: they usually offer a national helpline or text service. You may also need to research support options in the client's local area. Remember that clients who are using online or telephone services may very well prefer to access support networks online or by telephone.

When compiling your list, do contact the agencies or check their websites to ensure that you have up-to-date information, know their approximate waiting time, and understand their referral pathways – for example, can (or must) the client self-refer? And if therapist referrals are accepted, what information would the agency wish to receive from you?

If the client will have to wait for an appointment at the agency to which you are referring and you don't feel able to offer them full counselling sessions during this time, you could offer 'holding' sessions to help support them while they wait.

How to share information
Having referral information on hand allows you to send details to your client's device almost instantly. You can send the client links to organisations that offer support or specific services. Knowing how to send a link via text (in telephone counselling), email or app messaging is an essential skill to master, if you aren't already familiar with this.

If you are intending to share a client's information directly with an agency, then do ensure that you adhere to the Caldicott Principles, developed in 1997 following a review (chaired by Dame Fiona Caldicott) of how the NHS handled confidential patient information. Counselling professionals should have the confidence to share information in the best interests of their clients and within the framework set out by these principles, as well as being supported by the policies of their employers (if relevant) and professional bodies.

Building a colleague database
When considering referral to another practitioner, you would usually consider both training and experience in working with the client's presenting issues. You also have to consider their online skill set – are they competent to work with the issues via telephone, text, video etc.? The online technical skill set and experience of a practitioner are just as relevant as their other skills.

Building good relationships with the therapists to whom you might refer is the key to achieving smooth transitions and ethical referrals for your clients.

Inward referrals

Just as you might refer to other therapists, so you might receive referrals from others. So do think about your own (inward) referral pathways and what information you would need about a client being referred to you.

Questions to reflect on
- In what circumstances will you make a referral?
- How will you know what referral paths exist in your client's location?
- How will you judge the limits of your training and skill set?

Tasks to complete
- Build a list of referral pathways, revisiting them regularly to ensure they are up-to-date.
- Explore your own professional referral network, connecting with other counsellors that have specialist areas, and exploring the scope for mutual referrals.

Black-Hole Effect

We have all had the experience of sending an email or text, then waiting for a reply. When you wait and wait, and nothing comes back, it can feel almost like your message was sucked into a black hole, never to be acknowledged or returned! The term 'black-hole effect' was first coined by American psychologist John Suler (1997). It refers to the uncomfortable phenomenon of sending an email and never knowing whether or not it was received and read.

Psychological effects

Not receiving a response can lead to uncertainty in the sender, which may produce all kinds of thoughts and questions, for example those suggested by Suler (1997):

- Did the message get lost somewhere en route?
- Should I resend it, or would that just annoy them, make them feel guilty or put pressure on them – or make me look like I'm overly eager?
- Did the message actually arrive with them, but they haven't read it yet?
- Maybe they're away on holiday.
- Maybe they've got lots of emails and haven't had time to read mine yet.
- Am I that unimportant to them, that they would read all those other messages before mine?
- Maybe they're in trouble or hurt!
- Maybe they did read it but haven't yet replied: why?
- Don't I deserve a prompt reply? I'm busy too, you know!
- Maybe they're mad at me: did I write something that would make them that angry?
- Maybe they want to keep me sitting on the edge of my seat; maybe they're just toying with me. How dare they!
- Did I forget to press 'Send'? I'd better check my outbox.

As you can see, all kinds of emotions lie behind these reactions: fear, sadness, isolation, resentment, frustration, irritation and self-doubt, to name just some. Managing these requires good self-awareness in the counsellor; do consider personal therapy and/or journaling to work on these areas. If you notice these feelings in yourself, take them to supervision.

Consequences of the black-hole effect
The black hole can play on our subconscious angst by denying us the feeling of empowerment or security. It may even stir up primitive fears of being left behind. For clients, it can bring up fears of abandonment or despair, waiting for the counsellor to respond. For counsellors, it can leave you second-guessing whether you have somehow said or done something 'wrong' – a feeling of being deskilled.

Specific considerations in online counselling
Therapists who work solely via the medium of text or email may be more susceptible to the black-hole effect. A scenario where you are working online, then for some reason the client just 'disappears', fails to respond, and is never heard from again can cause anxious feelings in the therapist. This phenomenon can also manifest with telephone counselling, where the client abruptly ends or terminates therapy without notice.

You may be able to prevent the problem by thorough contracting, in which you should agree a backup communication method in the event that the primary method fails. Some clients may even be happy for you to have a family member's or friend's contact details as a backup.

If you assessed the person to be more likely to be at risk of harm to self, their sudden 'disappearance' may be even more concerning. Again, thorough contracting will ensure that you can, if you deem this justifiable in a particular situation, contact their GP or other relevant service.

> *Questions to reflect on*
> - How would you feel if a long-term client with whom you had been working 'disappeared' suddenly?
> - How will you make sure you don't send your client into a 'black hole'?
> - How will you manage their expectations regarding speed of response to emails and text messages?

> *Tasks to complete*
> - Think about your strategy on how to manage the black-hole effect.
> - Revisit your contract and put measures in place to manage the black-hole effect.
> - Journal about how you might feel and what you might think in the event of a client 'disappearing'.

Emergency Contacts

Working with clients in their own homes remotely can bring some specific risk issues. What would happen if a diabetic client slipped into a coma when you were speaking with them on the telephone, or if a client in distress disclosed that they had taken an overdose just before they came online for video-counselling? Taking no action is clearly not an option.

An emergency contact is someone you can speak with if the client is in danger. They can be:

- a friend
- a relative
- a professional who is working with the client, for example a community psychiatric nurse (CPN)
- the emergency services.

If the emergency contact is a relative or a friend, it is best if the client can tell them they are having therapy with you, so as to avoid confusion in the event of you needing to contact them. There may be times when you need to contact emergency services before you contact the relative/friend, e.g. if the client appears to be having a medical emergency.

Compiling an emergency contact list
It is essential that, when compiling an emergency contact list, you contract for this with the client. You must also keep the emergency contact details with you when working with the client so you can get help immediately if something goes wrong.

A contact list should include the name, address and telephone number of the emergency contact, their relationship to the client, and whether they know that the client is having therapy.

It can be difficult for a client who lives in a household where counselling is not well accepted, or where there is domestic violence, to provide an emergency contact. It is still important to discuss this during contracting, and to agree the most acceptable option in an emergency.

Using the emergency contact
If you need to speak with the emergency contact, share only

information that is relevant to the emergency. Be aware that some relatives or friends may be curious about what is being explored in therapy or what has happened in the client's personal life to trigger difficulties (e.g. self-harm). It is good practice to set your boundaries for information-sharing using the Caldicott Principles.

If you do have to use the emergency contact, ensure that you document this fully in your notes, including who you spoke to, when you spoke to them, and the content of the conversation.

> *Questions to reflect on*
> - How would you feel about contacting a relative if the client was in danger?
> - Do you understand the Caldicott Principles of information-sharing?

> *Tasks to complete*
> - Ensure that your contract captures an emergency contact, and include details about the importance and purpose of this.
> - Design your own emergency contact form.
> - Rehearse your emergency procedure with your buddy.

Risk Management

One of the challenges of online therapy is that you do not get as full a picture of the client as you would if you were seeing them face-to-face. Clients from certain groups may have behaviours or environments that contribute significantly to serious risk of harm to self or others. As noted in 'Suitability and Assessment', high-risk categories of clients include those presenting with eating disorders, personality disorders, severe mental-health conditions, risky behaviours (e.g. self-harm and suicidal thinking), domestic violence or addiction.

Unlike face-to-face work – where you can negotiate with a client to get some help if they disclose a life-threatening situation – working online poses several challenges. The most pressing of these is how we get help if the client becomes unwell during a session, expresses suicidal intent, or poses a danger to others in the household.

Risk management
A risk-management plan, also known as an 'intake form', allows you to identify any risks in advance, and so to help manage any clients who may be in danger. It is important to have a risk-management plan whether you are working face-to-face or online. This should form part of your contracting. It is best practice to revisit the risk-management plan regularly (as part of your reviews), and always to keep previous versions too, so as to ensure you have a complete audit trail of your actions. This helps protect both the client and you as a professional.

The information provides the basis of a risk assessment if you need to decide whether or not to break confidentiality. Areas to ask the client about are current medications (researching these if you are not familiar with them), underlying health issues, involvement with mental-health services and suicidal thoughts/plans/intent. The questions needed to elicit this information may feel very invasive, and it is therefore important to approach these in the right way, paying attention to your tone, and reminding the client of confidentiality and its limits. It also helps to explain why you need to collect this information.

As noted in 'Suitability and Assessment', it can be helpful to use standard mental-health questionnaires. As well as providing evidence-based information to support your decision-making on whether or not it is safe and ethical to work with a particular client, using a standard tool as part of your assessment for all clients can help reduce the feeling of invasiveness.

Just as we may still choose to work with suicidal clients face-to-face, having completed the necessary risk assessment (depending on our agency's policy, if relevant), it is possible to do so when working online. Some mental-health professionals do suggest avoiding working online (especially by telephone) with clients at risk, due to the reduced opportunity for visual and other cues, and the difficulty in safeguarding the client from a distance. Others, however, argue that online therapy may represent the potentially life-saving difference between a suicidal client opening up to someone or not (Jones and Stokes, 2009: 145).

The BACP (2019a: 9) advises:

> Care needs to be taken in communicating to clients what assistance can be offered from a distance in situations where the client becomes vulnerable or distressed or requires urgent support outside the scope of the service being

offered. It is good practice to have discussed with clients how they might be assisted before such a situation arises.

> *Questions to reflect on*
> - What do you need in a risk-management plan?
> - How will you use the information?

> *Tasks to complete*
> - Look at your risk-management policies and procedures, and amend them as needed.
> - Working with a buddy, practise how you deliver your intake form.

Boundaries

You will understand (from your face-to-face work) the need for boundaries. However, in the online world, boundaries can be crossed by the very nature of the technology we use. Boundaries help separate our working and private lives, which in turn helps us avoid overload, burnout and inappropriate relationships with clients. Unlike face-to-face work, the online world connects us to clients by the devices we carry around. This means we can be contacted at any time.

For telephone counselling, you may choose to get a second mobile phone (this can also help you keep work and home separate) – if you find smartphones challenging, you could choose to purchase a 'dumbphone' (i.e. a basic one that does not have internet functionality).

Being clear on when you are willing and able to be contacted is an essential element of contracting. Setting clear boundaries helps the therapist avoid burnout, and encourages the client to rely on their own ability to self-manage – so developing autonomy.

Areas to consider regarding online boundaries
Online boundaries include:

- clearly stating when you will be available and not available
- contracting for specific contact in the case of any client who is struggling
- making sure that your social-media accounts do not indicate when you are online
- avoiding using software that would show you are online (e.g. Skype)
- considering having a separate mobile-phone number for your work
- deciding whether you will have a voicemail service on your mobile number and, if so, thinking carefully what the message will say.

Specific considerations in online counselling
When working with vulnerable clients, it may be useful to consider offering a 15-minute 'check-in' call between sessions, and supplying the names and contact details of organisations that can offer immediate support (such as the Samaritans and Big White Wall).

Do remember the power of the disinhibition effect, including in yourself. The online world can be very immersive: so much so that therapists have been known to look up their clients' social-media profiles. Similarly, you may wish to secure your own social-media accounts, remembering that even if you disguise your name there, it is possible these days to use a photograph to do a reverse search, meaning your clients could still find you if you use a profile picture of yourself.

Transference and countertransference can be more problematic in telephone counselling, where you can hear the other person's voice but not see them. This can make it harder to differentiate between the actual person you are speaking to and the memory of someone from your past who reminds you of them. Similarly, the absence of visual information can lead to either party creating a fantasy sense of the other, and confusing this with reality.

It's also important to think about how you can try to prevent a client doing the following, and what you would do if they:

- failed to pay on time
- did not show up for their appointment
- recorded the session.

Questions to reflect on
- What structures do you need in place to make sure you can keep your boundaries?
- How will you communicate your boundaries to the client?
- What do you need in order to minimise the disinhibition effect on self?

Tasks to complete

- Consider how to manage unscheduled telephone calls, revisiting your response if a client tries to reach you between sessions.
- Ensure you have policies and procedures in place for when a client doesn't pay.
- Manage your online presence, looking at all your online profiles and privacy settings on social platforms.
- Journal about your thoughts and feelings around boundaries for working online.

Chapter 4

Transferring Skills Online

Effectiveness of Online Therapy

The concept of evidence-based practice began in the UK, where British doctor and researcher Professor Archie Cochrane noted in 1972 that most treatments selected by healthcare professionals for patients were not based on a systematic review of clinical evidence. Cochrane suggested international collaboration between researchers to develop systematic reviews of all the robust clinical trials. This exercise highlighted even further the gaps between research and clinical practice, and was the start of a general push for evidence-based practice throughout the NHS and wider healthcare system. The Cochrane Library today houses the Cochrane Reviews, as well as other healthcare databases.

Evidence-based practice is important because it aims to provide the most effective care, with the aim of improving outcomes. While the medical model is generally not a popular one in the world of counselling and psychotherapy, it nonetheless stands to reason that sharing and learning from good practice – including by being familiar with the research evidence – can help us provide the best possible service to our clients.

History of online counselling
Those who have researched the history of online therapy identify two significant events. The first was again in 1972, when

researchers at the University of California and Stanford University linked computers to facilitate a psychotherapy session. It is acknowledged that this was not a real psychotherapy session, more a proof of concept.

In 1986, Cornell University launched an online forum called 'Dear Uncle Ezra'. According to Lang (2007), writing in the *Cornell Chronicle*, Uncle Ezra is 'an anonymous Cornell staffer with a mental health background'.

Most observers would identify Dr David Sommers as the first therapist to use email and online chats with clients in different countries in 1995. He is also believed to be the first to offer fee-paying services online.

Counselling by telephone
In her doctoral thesis investigating the extent to which relational depth can be reached in online therapy, and the factors that facilitate and inhibit that experience, Treanor (2017: 17) noted that there is 'a substantial body of evidence which supports and shows the effectiveness of telephone-based support as a treatment option'.

Conclusion from research
Drawing on a comprehensive meta-analysis of the effectiveness of internet-based psychotherapeutic conducted by Barak et al. in 2008, Treanor (2017: 16) notes they found that 'Internet-based interventions are more effective in treating psychological problems such as PTSD [post-traumatic stress disorder], panic and anxiety, and less suited to treating physiological or somatic

disorders' and that 'young (19–24) and mid-range adults (25–39) seem to gain more from Internet-based therapy than youth (18 or younger) or older (40 or older) adults'.

Relational depth online

With regard to the possibility for developing relational depth when working online, Treanor (2017: 96) concludes that 'relational depth can be experienced by some individuals online while others are unable to reach that level of depth with their therapist despite experiencing it face-to-face'. This emphasises the importance of the therapist doing all they can to ensure that the client is suitable for online working.

The future

One area of technology that is being trailed is virtual reality (VR). The VR experience is known as 'immersive technology', and involves clients experiencing places and situations as if they were really there. Researchers have used VR for presenting issues such as anxiety and depression.

Questions to reflect on'
- How will the research impact your practice?
- What challenges does the research highlight?
- How do you envisage the future of online therapy?

Tasks to complete
- Ask your clients about their feelings around working online.
- Explore the research available and consider how you might apply this to your practice.

Telephone Counselling: Therapist Considerations

There are various considerations that are specific to telephone work, and some skills that are effective in face-to-face and online video-counselling may need to be adapted for telephone sessions, as a result of not being able to see the client. For example, it is challenging to show nonverbal communication when counselling by telephone, you will need to develop different ways of visually expressing the core conditions, and you may have to modify your core-model approach.

Your relationship with your telephone
The first thing to consider is the relationship you have with your device and the familiarity you feel when using it. Just as someone may struggle writing an essay on a computer that they usually use for playing games, a telephone therapist may find themselves slipping into patterns of informal conversation as if they were chatting to a friend. This relates in part to the disinhibition effect: the relative anonymity of both the client and the counsellor when using the telephone can change how we communicate.

Personality and the telephone
Whether or not you feel comfortable using the telephone may depend to an extent too on your personality and values. There seems to be anecdotal evidence that introverts often dislike the telephone as a means of communication, but the reasons given for this relate more to unexpected phone calls, which clearly does not apply to a planned therapy session. Indeed, introvert therapists may even find telephone counselling a better fit than forms of counselling that also involve visual cues, avoiding the risk of over-stimulation.

For those of us who struggle with the emphasis that society places on appearance, telephone counselling can offer a refreshing break from this. While the development of a non-judgemental approach is of course an intrinsic part of counselling training, do any of us manage not to experience any assumptions when we first see a new client? Our training should mean that we are aware of these, and so that they don't impinge on the development of the therapeutic relationship, but it can be refreshing in many ways to shed this whole area of concern.

On a related note, how a telephone-counselling client processes the lack of visual information on the therapist's appearance may also provide useful material for their therapy. For example, are they curious about your age, skin colour and other aspects of appearance? And how might you respond if they ask about such things?

Telephony skills
In recent years, the mobile phone has morphed into a handheld computer that delivers – among other things – a camera, diary, music/video player and fitness monitor. It has become relatively uncommon to use it to make telephone calls!

Using the telephone as a tool for therapeutic communication requires the development of a very specific skill set of enhanced listening and communication skills.

Using a headset
Using a headset is much more comfortable than holding the telephone to your ear for an hour, especially if you are working with three or four clients per day. Don't be tempted to use the loudspeaker function, as doing so can amplify background

sounds. This may leave the client feeling vulnerable, even though you are alone. If a client uses their loudspeaker function, you may miss what they say and need to ask for clarification.

Letting the client know you are listening
One of the key differences between working face-to-face and by telephone is the way the counsellor acknowledges what the client is saying. In face-to-face therapy, the counsellor's nonverbal communication can provide reassurance that the client has their full attention and is 'present'. Telephone counselling requires the therapist to confirm attention by the use of 'minimal encouragers' such as 'Aha', 'Yes', 'I see', 'Go on' and 'Hmmm'.

Working with silence
Because silence in a telephone conversation can mean that the other person has ended the call or been cut off, it is much harder to work with silence using this technology. When working face-to-face, seeing the client helps us understand the possible nature of a client's silence. But just as in face-to-face working, allowing the client time to finish reflecting or thinking is essential too when counselling by telephone. Don't be tempted to jump in and complete a client's sentence.

One useful way of working with silence is to remember the last thing you or the client said; this may provide a possible clue for the silence and an opportunity to check meanings and feelings when the client speaks again. Silences may be long, but when they end, do respond to the client in a supportive, empathic way.

Distance and dialect
Another challenge in working with a client over the telephone

is that of dialect. In face-to-face work, we may see clients from our local area, where dialect and intonation are more likely to be familiar to us. Working via telephone means that we may have clients outside our geographical area. As such, language may become a barrier. Sometimes dialects sound stronger over the telephone, so you may need to clarify what the client means.

Background noise
When both the client and the counsellor are in the same room, they have an appreciation of any background noise and can comment on the shared experience, e.g. noisy roadworks outside the building. When working on the telephone, you may not be able to assess how much noise the client is experiencing and so may need to check whether they can hear you.

If it sounds to you as if there is background noise at the client's end, you may need to take responsibility for addressing this. In particular, if it seems that another person may have entered the client's space, it is important to give the client the opportunity to acknowledge this and to end the call if they need to do so.

Anger and rage
One phenomenon observed in telephone counselling is that clients can get angry very quickly; this may again be a by-product of the disinhibition effect. If this happens, do reassure the client that it is acceptable to express emotion. Be aware that the client may not hear you the first time – so, if necessary, repeat the reassurance. Sometimes the client may project the anger on to you, for example saying: 'It's your fault this is happening.' If this happens, stay calm. Being defensive may fuel the fire.

Clients who talk non-stop
Sometimes, you may experience a client who talks and talks, not leaving any gap for you to reflect and paraphrase. One technique is to listen in silence and wait for the client to stop talking; the other is to talk over the client. Neither of these techniques is ideal and may be difficult for a counsellor to use. However, sometimes you may need to intervene if the client is confused or going around in circles.

Power and boundaries
Telephone counselling challenges a lot of the traditional views of the client–counsellor relationship. One area where this is noticeable is the balance of power – it tips in favour of the client as they can terminate the call instantly and never return. In some cases, clients can become abusive. It can be useful in a telephone-specific contract to build in a clause that covers termination of service in the event of this happening.

Visualising the core conditions
As in face-to-face work, the therapist's use of empathy, congruence and unconditional positive regard (UPR) provides the foundation for building and sustaining the therapeutic relationship. In telephone counselling, when you are expressive of your reactions, your client can hear how you physically empathise with what they have said. For example, you might make empathy visible as follows:

Client: Telling you about the abuse has made me feel vulnerable and alone again.
Counsellor: It feels like part of you is still experiencing feelings from the past. As I hear what you say, I

am leaning forward to be closer to you … I am here; you are not alone.

The therapist in this interaction is helping visualise the response a client would have seen in a face-to-face encounter. Similarly, the counsellor could visualise their nonverbal communication that indicates UPR as follows:

Client: So now I have told you. I went to prison for stealing from my employer. I feel so ashamed.

Counsellor: I hear what you say and the courage it took to say it. I do not have a shocked expression on my face. I am smiling warmly …

The words used by the counsellor to help the client see that the revelation did not bring a judgemental physical response. Last but not least, the counsellor can verbally mirror the client's nonverbal communication in the service of congruence and rapport. Notice how the use of the counsellor's language brings life into the interaction:

Client: So I told my boss I'm finally quitting my job – her face was a picture. I am waving my arms around doing a little dance as I tell you this.

Counsellor: I hear you – I am waving my arms around too, and jigging my feet.

Intuition and sense-strengthening
Rosenfield (2013: 94) brings into sharp relief the difference between face-to-face and phone counselling when she writes:

'I believe that many effective phone counselling responses are primarily intuitive. This can occur in a first session, although more often it will be in subsequent sessions once the counsellor has gained a greater sense of the client.'

Trusting the process is key, as Rosenfield (2013: 94) reflects in describing the intuitive process of nuanced listening:

> I listen to my gut instinct over my head and consider voice tone and nuances alongside words. Perhaps my capacity to empathize is greater in the non-visual mode or perhaps I am simply more willing to 'take a risk' with some of my responses because of the lack of visual information to support my thoughts. If I get it wrong the client corrects me and I feel it is important to go with my intuition.

When we use one of our senses more than another, we may very well neglect the others. Working without visual cues asks us to go back to the very basics of our practice – that of deep, nuanced listening. It also asks us not to be 'lazy' and not to presume from visual cues how the client is feeling. Instead, it invites a sense of vibrancy, asking us to explore – with thoughtful questions – what is happening in the relationship.

Other considerations
- Consider whether you wish to counsel on your mobile phone or landline.

- If using a mobile phone, always make sure your telephone is plugged in or sufficiently charged.
- If you tend to pace around while on the telephone, think about whether you will be able to attend fully while doing so, or whether you need to find a comfortable place where you can sit still.
- Make sure your service plan covers you for enough minutes of call time.
- Mute any notifications and other telephones in the room when you are in a session.
- Consider the power balance: whose 'minutes' are you using: yours or the client's? Clients on low income may be on a pay-as-you-go plan and be unable to afford the top-up credit for their mobile phone.

Questions to reflect on
- How do you view your telephone and what kind of calls do you usually make?
- How do you feel when making telephone calls, or at the prospect of doing so?
- How do you feel about working therapeutically on the telephone?
- How might you have to adapt your skills to telephone counselling?
- How will you manage any power imbalance between you and the client?
- What excites you about not relying on nonverbal cues?
- How will you adapt your questioning style?
- How will you balance curiosity and over-inquisitiveness in yourself?

> *Tasks to complete*
> - Undertake an audit of your telephone skills, including your visually expressive vocabulary. Plan how you will fill any gaps in these.
> - Practise your visualisation skills with your buddy.
> - Listen to skills sessions on YouTube (e.g. Carl Rogers and Gloria) without watching the video, and think about how it feels to hear the sound only – whether it adds or detracts from the session, and how it fits with you and your style.

Clients Seeing Themselves

Some clients may feel very challenged by the idea of seeing themselves on the screen. In order to reduce the chance of 'triggering' clients, it is important to be able to identify this in the initial assessment, and to identify possible solutions.

Fear of self

For some clients, seeing themselves reflected in a mirror or even a shop window can be an unpleasant or even a frightening experience. Clients with body dysmorphic disorder may struggle with self-image. It is not unknown for some clients to ask the therapist not to have any mirrors or reflective surfaces in the therapy room.

Making an assessment

Usually, clients will state a preference when they initially contact you for therapy. You can take this chance to discuss which service may be better suited to their needs. Sometimes, asking how clients feel about seeing themselves on screen can be quite revealing. They may prefer telephone counselling, or video with their camera turned off so they can see you but you cannot see them. It is useful to explore clients' preferences and concerns during the initial assessment.

Video skills

Sometimes, clients may not initially disclose that they have a fear of seeing themselves, and may then become triggered or uncomfortable during an online session. If this happens, you can – in some video-conferencing software – turn off the client's camera and see how they feel working audio-only. Or you can start the session without video cameras on, then turn one or both on if the client becomes comfortable with this. Some software will allow the client to minimise the video window that contains their image, so that it is tiny. This may be more manageable for some clients.

The key skill here is in how to control the video environment to meet the client's needs, just as you would when working face-to-face, e.g. switching the light on/off and adjusting the temperature. Make sure you know how to set a meeting up with the camera off as default, and how to switch off the client's video if they need you to do so.

A final option is to tell the client that you are stopping the meeting and will contact them by telephone; you could contract for this as a fall-back option.

Considerations in Text-Based Counselling

Text-based therapy can trace its roots back to the 1970s, but it came of age only with the birth of the internet. Therapy using text can come in many forms:

- *Internet Relay Chat* (IRC), better known as 'live chat' or a 'chat room', provides synchronous communication – that is, you can exchange conversation in real time.
- *Email* is a form of electronic letter, which needs to be received before a response can be sent. It is an asynchronous form of communication.
- *Short Message Service* (SMS) is the official term for texting using a mobile phone text. Text messaging is a form of asynchronous communication.

Many people use journaling as a way of processing their emotions, and text-based therapy draws on a similar concept.

It is possible to use text-based therapy alongside telephone or online therapy, drawing on the strengths of each to create a powerful hybrid.

Suitability for client and for therapist
One of the areas to bear in mind when considering working with text-based therapy is the issues it may bring up for the client. Clients who have had difficulties at school with written work – especially those with dyslexia or other specific learning difficulties – may be anxious when using written communication and so struggle with text-based therapy. As with all therapeutic approaches, find the best fit for the client.

Similarly, therapists should consider if they have the writing and reading skills to be able to work in a text-based environment.

Advantages of working by text
Text-based therapy offers a form of anonymity, which the client may prefer. It may also fit better into their schedule – especially in the case of asynchronous methods, where there is some flexibility around when messages are written. A text-based encounter may also suit clients whose internet culture favours this form of communication.

When a session is held in real time (i.e. synchronously), it allows the client to be more spontaneous, because they cannot edit out or restructure what they are saying, as they might do in email interaction. Working with live chat can sometimes help the therapist gain clarity or insight into what is going on with the client.

Disadvantages of working by text
Confidentiality can be an issue when working by text. For example, when working with online chat (synchronous), you may have to consider whether the client is using a shared computer. Your conversation may be found by someone looking up the client's internet history. Also, clients may just stop communicating if a third party comes into the room.

Jones (2008: 64) offers some crucial observations on 'beginnings' in text-based encounters:

> The typing ability and speed of both client and counsellor could be an issue … If either of you type very slowly, then the conversation can become protracted and not flow easily. Initially, both of you may find that you are taking care to type correctly, concentrating on spelling and punctuation, rather than on the meaning you are trying to convey.

Difference between email/text and live chat
When you are working in real time, you can be more spontaneous, and get an insight into what is going on. There is an opportunity to clarify the meaning of the client's words and work through any misunderstandings. When working via email or text, you need to consider the context of what is being said, and that the client cannot respond in real time.

Text-based ethics

When you have finished an online text session or an email interaction, it may be useful to ask the client if they wish to have a copy of the transcript. Clients may find this helpful to reread, helping them process your joint work.

Writing the initial email

Here is a possible response to a client who wishes to have therapy by email:

 You can download this example from within the free online companion course by visiting counsellingtutor.com/online

Response to Client for Email Counselling

Hello Jane

Thank you for returning the signed agreement. I am glad to have the opportunity of working with you.

I am delighted to offer you three counselling exchanges through email; as you mention, this method seems to suit you best.

I have noted that you have provided quite a bit of information regarding where you are at in the agreement. Thank you for being so thorough.

I will send your first email in reply to the information you have provided by no later than the evening of Thursday 1st November. This will be our first exchange.

I note you have indicated that you are available most days. Would you feel comfortable getting your emails to me by a Tuesday evening and my reply would then be with you by the following Thursday evening? If this suits you, our second exchange will be in the week commencing 5th November, and our third and final exchange in week commencing 12th November.

If these arrangements do suit you, then there is no need to reply to this email. If the arrangements do not suit you or if you have any questions arising from this email, please feel free to reply. I will try my best to answer your questions or to make an alternative arrangement for our exchanges. Thank you again for taking the time to get in touch.

Kind regards

Tom

Note how the therapist acknowledges the initial contact with the client and the issues they wish to bring, and also the clarity about when they will receive and need to respond to emails. For the client, revealing their emotions to you in writing may seem exposing, and if they don't know when to expect a response, they may be waiting on tenterhooks, worrying about the content of their own email.

How to structure an email session
Responding to a text-based or email interaction requires you to abandon the usual way of writing and to use a different approach.

In a standard email exchange (e.g. with friends), we tend to reply to the email as a whole, in one block of text, and perhaps not pick up on each individual point. In text-based counselling, it is good practice for the therapist to use a different colour, style or weight of font, and to reply to each statement or paragraph individually, placing each response within the body of the client's email, underneath the statement it relates to. This creates a feeling of being in a conversation together. The case study below illustrates this technique.

 You can download this example from within the free online companion course by visiting counsellingtutor.com/online

Email Exchange – Example

Hi Susan, I've placed my reply to you within the text of your email as I feel this helps me to respond more spontaneously than writing a separate reply. If you would prefer me to write separately next time, please let me know. I apologise in advance if it feels like I ask a lot of questions in this first reply. I do this to gain a more in-depth sense of things you mention and to understand how you are feeling.

Dear Trish, I'm feeling a bit stuck about what to say, to be honest. I don't normally share my feelings much and this issue seems especially hard to talk about. That's why I chose email counselling, as I was hoping it'd be easier to write about but I'm still struggling to get started.

Sometimes, people find it easier to say it in writing than face-to-face with someone. So I think I understand why you may have chosen email counselling as a preferred option to face-to-face counselling.

I'm feeling really down at the moment – it's a familiar feeling to me. It's bad enough feeling this way but then I have this habit of making it all even worse by looking for comfort in stuff that isn't good for me. Like sometimes I overeat, or start smoking again. Or I might go overboard on wine. I always end up feeling gross – like I've spoilt my health and worrying too that anyone who sees me can tell what I've been doing. I feel ashamed.

Can I ask how your current state of health is to help give me a sense of the kind of support you might need? Also can you tell me if your current ways of seeking comfort have begun recently or if there is a pattern that you recognise from past experiences?

When I'm going through a stressful time, like I am at the moment with all the changes at work, I kind of lose interest in being healthy and just neglect myself really. It's like I have no control over it. And the short-term gain feels good – I love the feeling of eating loads of fried and sugary food, of feeling chilled after a packet of cigarettes or a bottle of wine. I really need that at the time. But then – when the buzz wears off – I'm left feeling so dirty and guilty. Like I've really let myself down, and messed up my body. I really want to make changes, so I just don't do it in the first place.

I can hear that it's feeling like a vicious circle at the moment – feeling bad about life, looking for comfort in unhealthy habits, but then feeling bad about yourself too afterwards. It sounds hard to break out of.

I've been looking at some websites for advice, and there are lots of activities, suggestions and stuff that help you look at how to break the cycle and think more positively about yourself, and they do help me. But it's hard finding time to do these things, and it's even more difficult trying to think positively about myself when I look and feel so ugly and unhealthy. I hate how I must look to other people. When anyone focuses on me, I just want the earth to open up.

I'm really sorry that you're feeling that way. Can I ask what makes you feel ashamed and embarrassed when people focus on you, as I'm not clear whether you feel they're looking at your body – or you as a person – negatively?

Another thing that I'm worried about is that it'll soon be New Year – another year over – and I feel really worried that my life is slipping away without me being anywhere near to where I want to be. I always used to think that by this age I'd be married and have a good job, nice house, kids etc. but none of those things has happened for me. I know what I want, but I just can't get there. And in the meantime, the time – the years – are just slipping through my fingers somehow, while I eat, drink, smoke, wreck my body and feel sorry for myself. What a waste.

I'm not sure what you feel is changing, or will change by you becoming older. I get the sense that you are feeling under pressure in some way to be or do something specific both professionally and personally – am I right in this?

Yes, I do feel a kind of pressure, and it's worse since moving away from the village where I grew up. I thought I'd feel better in a new place, and have the chance of new opportunities and new people to meet, but it's just not been happening for me. Life's not turning out how I thought, and that gets to me.

Do you have the support of your family in settling in to a new way of living and a new place? It sounds as though the place where you grew up was very different from here in the city.

I have made some new friends here, and one of them is planning a New Year's Eve party. I really want to go but am worried I'll come over all morose and emotional at midnight again and end up spoiling the fun by weeping on everyone. So I'm just going to stay at home.

It sounds from what you have said that this has happened before on other New Year's Eves. Can you explain this a little further in your next email and perhaps consider why New Year stands out for you as a time when you feel so sad or distressed?

I've tried to tell them how I don't like New Year, how I'm trying to be healthier and to feel more cheerful, but they just joke that we all need to let our hair down sometimes. I don't think they have any clue about how the ache I have inside.

I was wondering if you were able to ask whether anyone would like to spend New Year's Eve together differently

– something that you feel you would be more comfortable with. I'm thinking that although everyone is saying they're looking forward to the party, some of them might also be wishing they could do something a bit quieter.

I think that's it for now. Writing this has made me feel a bit better, I guess. It's good to get it off my chest, especially since it's been bottled up for so long. At the same time, it's horrible seeing my problems staring back at me on the page as I write this, admitting that something is genuinely becoming an issue, instead of just ignoring it and hoping it will go away. I want it to go away, but I want to get rid of it myself. I want to take control of things again, like it used to be when I was young.

I'm glad that you have felt comfortable to tell me how you are feeling, and I understand that when it's written down it can feel very 'concrete' as opposed to something that can be ignored. I think that you are also very courageous to have sought help in 'getting back the control' you are seeking with the habits you want to change.

It would be helpful for me in understanding how you're feeling if you were to tell me more about your life, particularly family and early life experiences, as well as current ones, in your next email.

I would also suggest checking out this website, Get Self Help, if you haven't already seen it, as it offers a good range of support with issues relating to how to break vicious cycles of the type you've described. It's at https://www.getselfhelp. co.uk/. Let me know what you think of it.

I look forward to hearing from you again in your next email.

Best wishes

Trish

Know your netiquette
Working online brings with it a specific approach to social norms known as 'netiquette'. The word, first used in the 1980s, is a combination of the words 'net' and 'etiquette'; it describes the socially acceptable way to use the internet – for example, respecting other users' views and being courteous when interacting with people online.

Examples of counselling netiquette include the following:

- Think carefully about the colour you choose for your responses to clients' statements, making sure this is legible but non-threatening. For example, red would not be a good colour to choose (it signals danger in many cultures, and may also trigger transference from school days, when teachers may have used this colour to correct work); green can work well, generally being seen as a neutral, accepting colour.
- Avoid using all-capitals as this can suggest that you are SHOUTING!

- Read back over your responses before sending them to remove any errors; having lots of slips may look unprofessional and give the client the impression that you have rushed your response to them.

Questions to reflect on
- How do you feel about text-based therapy?
- What are your strengths and limitations in this area?
- How will your text-based work be supervised?

Task to complete
- Practise text interactions with your buddy.

Chapter 5

Working Professionally Online

Online Business Presence

It is important to be able to convert your online mindset to an online presence by:

- positively promoting your online practice
- understanding what clients may look for in an online therapist
- seeing the link between having a positive view of online therapy and developing your practice.

In short, your online presence should reflect your online mindset, promoting a positive and confident view of your online practice. As most qualified therapists have a website and advertise on some form of therapy directory, taking the opportunity to promote yourself as a competent online practitioner is essential. Promoting your practice can be achieved in several ways.

A high-quality picture
It is said that a picture paints a thousand words. This definitely holds true when offering your services online. A good-quality picture of yourself – perhaps even one taken professionally, if this is affordable for you – serves three important functions:

- It shows the online client who you are, so they can put a face to the voice on the telephone or the text/email.
- It shows that they will be working with a real human, ready to hear their story.
- It can reduce the 'online fantasy' effect, where a client may become distracted or fantasise about their therapist (a form of transference).

Do ensure that your photo is up-to-date – so you may need to change it if you change your appearance in a noticeable way (e.g. grow a beard or change your hair style/colour markedly). If you use an out-of-date picture, your client may be surprised by your appearance when they first 'meet' you online.

It is also important to think about the background for your photo, and for your online working, ensuring – as you would when working face-to-face – that no family pictures and other items are on show that would reveal more about you personally than might be helpful. Some counsellors who work online choose to maintain a consistent background by, for example:

- always sitting in the same location for online sessions
- having a curtain or other backdrop that they use as a consistent background for their online sessions
- using the feature on some video-conferencing software packages (e.g. Zoom) where you can set a photograph (perhaps of your therapy room at its cleanest and tidiest!) as a constant background. As noted in 'Online Confidentiality', if you do use this, practise with it before speaking to your client, as

sometimes it can visually 'cut off' parts of you, which could appear strange and disconcerting to clients.

Show your commitment
When you describe your practice on your website or on any form of sales page, try to put yourself in the client's shoes. Consider the questions they may want to ask, and answer them. Be as passionate about your online practice as you are about your face-to-face face work.

Google yourself
Your clients almost certainly will! It may seem like an odd thing to do. However, you may be surprised at your internet footprint. Old social-media accounts or outdated information may give the clients more information than you want them to have. It is also a good idea to check the settings on your social-media accounts, so you control who sees any content.

Questions to reflect on
- Have your perceptions of online work changed since you began reading this book – and if so, how?
- Where are you now with your learning about online counselling?
- What else do you need to know?

Tasks to complete
- Consider all your online activity, your social-media accounts and review your privacy settings for each platform.
- Think about what opportunities you see opening up with regard to online practice.

Supervision

While you will be well used to receiving clinical supervision for your face-to-face counselling practice, you may need to adjust how you use supervision in order to get the best from this when working in an online environment. For example, your supervision needs may change, and you may need to integrate online-specific theories into supervision. You may even decide to receive your supervision online, and realise certain benefits from this.

Finding a supervisor for online work
If your existing supervisor doesn't have experience of – and qualifications in – working online, you may feel the need to find a new supervisor for your new practice. Ideally, supervisors should have a working knowledge of medium-specific theories before supervising those who practise in this way. For example, a supervisor who doesn't work online themselves may be unfamiliar with the disinhibition and the black-hole effects. Safeguarding also brings very different challenges when working online.

If you will still be working both face-to-face and online, you could do either of the following:

- keeping your current supervisor for online work and have a second for online work. (ensuring that the time spent on the two together totals at least the required minimum for your professional body – usually 1.5 hours per month).

- Move to a new supervisor who can cover both/all areas of practice. If you are not yet qualified as a counsellor, it may be more sensible to have just one supervisor, as it will be more straightforward to have one person to sign off your placement hours.

Applying theory in supervision

Working in an online environment is a specific discipline, and requires clients to adapt to a very different way of interacting with you. The online environment also requires you to consider new theories, and how they apply to both your clients and your own process. It is important that your supervisor has enough knowledge of online theory and practice to be able to support you.

In addition to all the usual components of clinical supervision, it may be useful to set aside some time for 'reflecting on the medium'. After all, whatever technology you are using will act as a 'phenomenological filter' between you and the client.

Being supervised online

If you are delivering therapy online, would you consider being supervised in the same medium? It could be argued that if you are working via telephone or email, you should be supervised in the same way, thereby 'talking the talk and walking the walk'.

We include below a checklist for using technology in clinical supervision (CCPA, 2019: 33–35).

Using Technology in Clinical Supervision

One of the main benefits of online supervision is increased access to high-quality supervision regardless of location, including to supervisors with specific expertise that might not otherwise be available to you.

As well as all the usual ethical guidelines that would apply to face-to-face clinical supervision, there are specific areas to consider if you are intending to offer or receive online supervision.

If you are seeking supervision, you should consult only with someone who has experience and training in working online. It can be helpful to be supervised using the same technology in which you are working.

Choice of technology
Technologies for clinical supervision include:

- face-to-face
- telephone (landline or mobile)
- digital/video recording that is shared with supervisor
- video-conferencing
- text or live chat
- email.

Choose the technology that best meets the needs of the

supervisee (as long as the supervisor is also comfortable with this), taking into consideration:

- availability
- affordability
- reliability
- privacy
- security
- effect of the technology on the working alliance.

Supervision contract

Informed consent for the supervisee needs to include:

- how information will be kept confidential
- how to communicate in case of a technical failure
- limitations of the technology
- potential risks of the technology
- potential benefits of the technology
- emergency plan for client crisis
- social-media policy.

The following areas should be discussed between the supervisor and supervisee:

- signing and adhering to a clinical supervision contract
- challenges of using technology and how it may impact on communication, e.g. your and the client's perceptions of an acceptable length of silence before initiating conversation
- minimising distractions and avoiding unrelated multi-tasking during supervision time

- when to use face-to-face or telephone contact to discuss sensitive information
- social-media policy
- shared responsibility for maintaining privacy and security
- whether additional supervision time may be required.

Knowledge and skills required

Supervisors should have the following knowledge and skills, and demonstrate the following good practice, in using technology in clinical supervision:

Knowledge
- current types of technology and their potential uses
- pros and cons of different technology platforms, and how to select an appropriate one
- how to minimise risk associated with transferring and storing sensitive data
- suitable reading material on professionalism, privacy/ security and ethics regarding technology
- implications of technology for supervisors and supervisees
- vicarious liability
- potential disinhibition effects on both the supervisor and supervisee
- current legislation and the professional ethics of the supervisee's ethical body

Skills
- using technology in general to at least a basic level
- using the specific technology to be applied
- applying privacy settings appropriately

- troubleshooting any common problems in both general and specific technology

Good practice
- protecting client privacy and confidentiality
- screening the supervisee's appropriateness to receive supervision via distance methods, and ensuring that the supervisee screens clients
- translating best practices in clinical supervision to the technology-based format.

Using different technologies in clinical supervision
For all modalities, discuss personal data only if the technology is secure, is password-protected, and has been vetted by you for compliance with the GDPR.

Synchronous methods
- Conduct calls only in a private office where you cannot be overheard.
- Use a headset to improve sound quality and privacy.
- Avoid using public or unsecured Wi-Fi for calls on a mobile phone.
- Have a backup communication plan in case of technical failure.
- Limit distractions.
- If using live chat, practise your writing skills so that you can communicate clearly and concisely.

Asynchronous methods
Clarify with your supervisor/supervisee whether it is acceptable

to text or email them at any time, or whether they have preferred days/times to receive such communications.

Digital video or audio recordings
- Ensure security protocols are in place for recording, transmitting, archiving and destroying the recording.
- For video recordings, have the camera on the counsellor only.

Email
- Encrypt all emails.
- Pay attention to tone, and learn ways to compensate for the lack of visual cues.

File-sharing
- Thoroughly vet any cloud-based storage for compliance with the GDPR.
- Ensure that both sending and receiving devices are also GDPR-compliant.
- Use encryption software to share files.
- Use passwords and the highest privacy settings.
- Consider screen-sharing.

Text messaging
- Use this only for simple, non-confidential conversations.
- Practise using this mode of communication for clarity and brevity.

Self-Care

During training, counsellors learn about self-care and boundaries. Taking care of self means that we try to achieve a healthy work–life balance, which in turn allows us to offer our clients a high-quality service. Self-care also extends longevity in work by preventing burnout or becoming jaded. Online counselling presents some specific challenges to self-care.

Transference in telephone counselling
When counselling by telephone, transference and countertransference can increase, as McLeod (2013: 553) explains:

> There does, however, appear to be one important process dlmension along which telephone counselling differs from face-to-face work ... The faceless helper is readily perceived as an 'ideal' and can be imagined to be anything or anyone the caller needs or wants.

Denied the opportunity of seeing the person they are talking to, clients (and therapists) may subconsciously fantasise about the person on the end of the telephone.

Screen time

For counsellors working via video, taking account of your screen time is essential. Research has shown that the use of computer monitors can affect health and sleep patterns. The Sleep Foundation (2020) observes: 'The blue light that's emitted from these screens can delay the release of sleep-inducing melatonin, increase alertness, and reset the body's internal clock (or circadian rhythm) to a later schedule.'

If you are working on a screen a lot, do ensure too that you have a regular eye test.

Wired for sound

If you counsel via telephone, you may wish to consider volume levels and the quality of the headset you are using, as both can exacerbate hearing loss. Trebilcock (2020) points out:

> In the UK, hearing loss affects one in six adults, according to an NHS report. And last year, the World Health Organization (WHO) warned that more than one billion people worldwide are at risk due to unsafe listening … The NHS [2018] recommends that you listen at no more than 60% of the maximum volume on your device, and to not use earphones or headphones continuously for more than an hour at a time, taking a break of at least five minutes every hour.

Taking breaks

Taking a break is also important to avoid joint stiffness and discomfort: we can really seize up if we are sitting working in a set position for long periods. Think too about your sitting position while counselling online or by telephone, ensuring that you aren't always angling your neck upwards or downwards, or having to hold a telephone to your ear.

It is generally thought that longer breaks are needed between clients when working online or by telephone than face-to-face. Remember too that – just as it takes time to build fitness at a sport you haven't so far trained in regularly – so it takes time to build up stamina in online and telephone counselling.

Never leaving work

Working from home can impact on self-care. Where does work begin and end? The online world is 24/7/365: it never stops. It may be worth remembering that even Sigmund Freud had a separate part of his house where he saw 'patients' (as he called them). Setting a healthy work–life balance is essential in the world of online counselling.

Questions to reflect on
- How will you introduce self-care related to the technology you use in supervision?
- What boundaries will you revisit before working in an online environment?

Task to complete
- Consider the time slots you have available for online therapy sessions and ensure you have allowed for regular breaks.

Endings

Ending individual counselling sessions

When a client attends a face-to-face counselling session, we take care to prepare them to be able to leave calmly, doing our best to start to bring them out of very deep emotions in time for them to travel home safely and to re-enter their everyday life. The period of time between leaving our room and arriving in their next destination may add to this, serving in itself as a useful transition from therapy back to the demands of everyday life.

When working online or by telephone, however, the client may literally walk away from their screen and into the next room, where their colleagues, partner and/or children may bombard them with demands. It is therefore important to begin the preparation for ending a session earlier in online and telephone counselling than in face-to-face work; you might also like to ask the client at the end of the session what they will be doing next, as a way to support the transition.

If the people they will next come into contact with are aware that they are having counselling, you may wish to talk to the client (as early as contracting stage) about what they might be able to do to explain their post-session needs to those people – for example, asking their partner to be particularly considerate and gentle towards them when they first 'emerge' from a session. Some clients may like to be asked how their session went, while others may prefer not to discuss it: again, it can be helpful for clients to discuss and agree this with those close to them.

The same applies to you too, as the counsellor: do ensure that you prepare for – and express your needs regarding – your own transition from online and telephone work back into your personal life.

Ending a course of counselling
A course of therapy can come to an end in various ways. There are typically three ways in which this happens:

- *The agreed ending* – where both the client and the counsellor meet to conclude the therapeutic journey. It's a time to reflect and take stock of the changes or new awareness the client has gained. This type of ending is usually the most satisfying for both parties, as it leads to a sense of a task completed.
- *The one-sided ending* – where the client unilaterally leaves therapy without any warning. This may be difficult for the therapist to process, as the finality may lead to feelings of resentment or loss. One-sided endings can also impact the therapist's confidence as they may bring up feelings of inadequacy. For those using telephone or text, this can be amplified by the black-hole effect.
- *The unavoidable ending* – where therapy comes to an end because the client becomes ill or has financial difficulties. Or you, as the counsellor, may be able to offer only a fixed amount of sessions, and the client may be unhappy at therapy coming to an end.

Whatever the reason for the ending, don't underestimate the feelings that may come up for you and your client. It is also worth considering that emotions around endings may be amplified when working by text, email or telephone due to the transferential nature of not seeing the client.

Considerations in agreed endings
Endings should prove to be a positive experience, which – once experienced – may be replicated in other areas of the client's life. A good ending should feel like a 'graduation', that of a task complete. It leaves the client ready to engage with the next stage of life's journey, and leaves the therapist feeling they have given enough.

Endings should be prepared for from the very beginning of counselling, including in contracting, and should be revisited in reviews. If you work in a service that offers a set number of sessions, you may like to remind the client in each session how many more they have left. As the client approaches the final stage of counselling, it can be helpful to explore how the client feels about ending, and whether there are any referrals you need to put in place or any signposting you can provide. It can also be helpful to let clients know how and when they can refer back in future.

Questions to reflect on
- When you leave a social function or a gathering, how and when do you leave?
- How can you use your answer to the above question to learn about how you may approach endings in the counselling context?
- What kinds of endings leave you feeling uncomfortable?

Evaluation Forms

The main purposes for evaluation in counselling are to:

- see whether your client's expectations have been met
- discover your client's experience of the process
- monitor any client dissatisfaction
- help develop your practice
- discover any 'blind spots' or areas for personal development.

How to instigate the evaluation process

At the end of therapy, ask the client whether they would be willing to fill in an evaluation form. You can send them a form by email and ask them to return it to you completed. The difficulty with this is that you may not get honest answers, as the client may feel they cannot tell you the truth (since it will be obvious who has submitted it).

Another way is to create an online evaluation form that the client can fill in anonymously within, say, two months. If you have a busy practice, this gives time for the answers you receive not to be easily linked to any particular client.

You can create online evaluation forms using several free software packages such as:

- Google Forms
- SurveyMonkey
- GetFeedback
- KwikSurveys.

You create your survey, then email a link to the client; they then fill it in and submit it online. Together, the results build up a picture of the effectiveness of your practice, and what areas you may wish to develop.

Possible questions
Do explain and introduce the survey and its purpose at the start. For example, you might write something like this.

> It is particularly important to me to assess the impact and quality of the service I provide. I would appreciate you taking a few minutes to give me feedback on the service you received from me. I am happy to have both positive and negative feedback, so please feel free to give me your honest views.

Some questions might be multiple-choice ones, where the client chooses one or more answers from a set list, for example focusing on:

- to what extent counselling has helped the client overall (the possible answers here might be 'A lot', 'To a limited extent' and 'Not at all')

- to what extent counselling has helped the client reach the goal that they decided at the start of the sessions (again, the possible answers might be 'A lot', 'To a limited extent' and 'Not at all')
- in what ways the client thinks you have helped them (with answers such as 'Listened to me', 'Understood how I was feeling', 'Understood what my situation was', 'Gave me useful information', 'Helped me to explore my concerns', 'Helped me to rethink how I do things', 'Referred me to another service' and 'Not applicable')
- whether the client would recommend the counselling service to a friend ('Yes' or 'No').

Other questions might ask the client to write in their own answers, in the forms of comments, for example:

- describing in more detail the ways in which counselling helped them
- listing any ways in which they found counselling overall or any particular aspects of the service unhelpful.

Considerations when using online evaluation forms
When using an online evaluation form, consider the following:

- Do not ask your client to provide any contact or identifiable details.
- Read the confidentiality policies of the company you are using.
- Remember that anonymous feedback plays into the disinhibition effect!

Questions to reflect on
- What kind of feedback do you want to gather and why?
- How will you deal with any negativity?

Tasks to complete
- Have a look at different survey tools available online.
- Using self-reflection, consider how you can develop yourself in your practice.

Chapter 6

Moving Forward with Online Counselling

Developing as an Online Professional

As counselling professionals, we never stop learning. Indeed, CPD is a required part of being a registered member of the BACP and other professional bodies in the field of counselling and psychotherapy. Ongoing development includes honing your skills, developing your ethical practice, understanding the use of technology, and adapting your modality to the online world. As technology is changing all the time, it's really important that we keep our technical skills up-to-date.

We hope you have enjoyed this book, and having worked your way through it – including reflecting on the various questions and completing all the tasks – is a huge achievement. But of course, the learning doesn't stop – and this is really the beginning of the journey as opposed to the end. So do revisit the book when you need a refresher – and consider what additional learning you may need and wish to gain in order to work online in the very best service of your clients.

For example, you might want to consider training in a smaller group, where you can hone your practical skills with observation and feedback from a specialist tutor. Or you might like to think about specialising in a specific client group (such as children and young people) or client presentation (e.g. bereavement). You may even be thinking about doing a master's degree or a doctorate. If so, online therapy could be a very relevant topic to investigate – perhaps outcomes compared to face-to-face work, the experience of older people in therapy, or clients' phenomenological view of being counselled in their own environment.

Future of Online Therapy

Carl Rogers spoke of a dawning 'world of tomorrow' that would produce 'persons of tomorrow'. And we're sure that if he was here, he would be really excited about online counselling. By committing your time to learning about online therapy, you are showing yourself to be a person of tomorrow!

We can't know in what direction exactly online therapy will develop. There are lots of interesting and innovative ideas out there – for example, working with VR. Who knows: we may one day be putting on our VR headsets and sitting down in a virtual counselling room to work with our clients there.

What we do know is that online counselling has well and truly come of age, and it's likely that clients will increasingly want online counselling. For example, clients who are housebound or find it difficult to travel to see a counsellor face-to-face are likely to welcome online work. Online therapy could also be invaluable for those who have to travel a lot – whether on business or for personal reasons.

So congratulations to you, because you are a pioneer of a new frontier in counselling!

Bibliography and Further Reading

Adlington J (2009) *Online Therapy – Reading between the Lines: A practical NLP based guide to online counselling and therapy skills*, MX Publishing

Amichai-Hamburger Y, Brunstein Klomek A, Friedman D, Zuckerman O & Shani-Sherman T (2014) 'The future of online therapy', *Computers in Human Behavior*, 41, 288–294: https://www.idc.ac.il/he/research/arl/Documents/publications/The_future_of_online_therapy.pdf

Anthony K & Merz Nagel D (2010) *Therapy Online: A Practical Guide*, Sage

BACP (2018) *Ethical Framework for the Counselling Professions*, BACP: https://www.bacp.co.uk/events-and-resources/ethics-and-standards/ethical-framework-for-the-counselling-professions/

BACP (2019a) Good Practice in Action 047 – *Fact Sheet: Working online in the counselling professions*, BACP: https://www.bacp.co.uk/media/2162/bacp-working-online-supplementary-guidance-gpia047.pdf

BACP (2019b) Good Practice in Action 091 – *Fact Sheet: Working with interpreters in the counselling professions*, BACP: https://www.bacp.co.uk/media/6514/bacp-working-with-interpreters-fact-sheet-gpia091-jul19.pdf

Barak A, Hen K, Boniel-Nissim & Shapira N (2008) 'A Comprehensive Review and a Meta-Analysis of the Effectiveness of Internet-Based Psychotherapeutic Interventions', *Journal of Technology in Human Services*, 109–160: https://www.tandfonline.com/doi/abs/10.1080/15228830802094429

Canadian Counselling and Psychotherapy Association (2019) *Guidelines for Uses of Technology in Counselling and Psychotherapy*, CCPA: https://www.ccpa-accp.ca/wp-content/uploads/2019/04/TISCGuidelines_Mar2019_EN.pdf.

Carroll M & Gilbert M (2011) *On Being A Supervisee: Creating Learning Partnerships*, Vukani Publishing

Childress C (2000) 'Ethical Issues in Providing Online Psychotherapeutic Interventions', *Journal of Medical Internet Research*, Jan-Mar; 2(1): e5: https://www.ncbi.nlm.nih.gov/pmc/articles/PMC1761841/

Etherington K (2016) 'Personal experience and critical reflexivity in counselling and psychotherapy research', *Counselling & Psychotherapy Research*, Volume 17, Issue 2: 85–94: https://onlinelibrary.wiley.com/doi/abs/10.1002/capr.12080 [full article available to BACP members via the online members' portal at https://www.bacp.co.uk/bacp-journals/counselling-and-psychotherapy-research-journal/]

Foster C (2020) *What Is the Disinhibition Effect?* Sussex Rainbow Counselling: https://www.sussexrainbowcounselling.com/post/what-is-the-disinhibition-effect?

Green D (2005) *Ground Rules in Online Psychotherapy* (doctoral thesis): http://www.psychom.com/Onlinehistory_en.html

ICO (2020) *Age appropriate design: a code of practice for online services*, ICO: https://ico.org.uk/for-organisations/guide-to-data-protection/key-data-protection-themes/age-appropriate-design-a-code-of-practice-for-online-services/

Jones G & Stokes A (2008) *Online Counselling: A Handbook for Practitioners*, Palgrave

Lang S (2007) 'For two decades, Dear Uncle Ezra, world's first online advice column, has aided the perplexed, the shy and the confused', *Cornell Chronicle*: https://news.cornell.edu/stories/2007/02/any-person-any-question-ask-dear-uncle-ezra-advice

Maples-Keller J, Burnel B, Sae-Jin K & Rothbaum B (2017) 'The use of virtual reality technology in the treatment of anxiety and other psychiatric disorders, *Harvard Review of Psychiatry*, May–June, 25(3), 103–113: https://www.ncbi.nlm.nih.gov/pmc/articles/PMC5421394/

McLeod J (2013) *An Introduction to Counselling*, Open University Press

Membrey D & Mitchels B (2019) 'Demystifying GDPR', *Private Practice*, BACP: https://www.bacp.co.uk/bacp-journals/private-practice/march-2019/demystifying-gdpr/

Mozer E, Franklin B & Rose J (2008) 'Psychotherapeutic intervention by telephone', *Clinical Interventions in Aging*, June, 3(2): 391–396: https://www.ncbi.nlm.nih.gov/pmc/articles/PMC2546483/

National Sleep Foundation (2020) *How Blue Light Affects Kids and Sleep:* https://www.sleepfoundation.org/articles/how-blue-light-affects-kids-sleep

NHS (2018) *5 Ways to Prevent Hearing Loss*, NHS: https://www.nhs.uk/live-well/healthy-body/top-10-tips-to-help-protect-your-hearing/

NHS (2019) *Overview: Consent to Treatment*, NHS: https://www.nhs.uk/conditions/consent-to-treatment/

North M & North S (2018) 'The Sense of Presence Exploration in Virtual Reality Therapy', *Journal of Universal Computer Science*, vol. 24, no. 2: 72–84: http://www.jucs.org/jucs_24_2/the_sense_of_presence/jucs_24_02_0072_0084_north.pdf

Pelkey J (2007) *Entrepreneurial Capitalism and Innovation: A History of Computer Communications 1968–1988*: http://www.historyofcomputercommunications.info/

Richards D (2009) 'Features and benefits of online counselling: Trinity College online mental health community', *British Journal of Guidance and Counselling*, August, 37(3):231–242: https://www.researchgate.net/publication/214499448_Features_and_benefits_of_online_counselling_Trinity_College_online_mental_health_community

Richards D & Viganò V (2012) Online Counseling, in *Encyclopedia of Cyber Behavior* (edited by Yan Z), IGI Global: https://www.researchgate.net/publication/215572313_Online_Counseling

Rosenfield M (2013) *Telephone Counselling: A Handbook for Practitioners*, Palgrave

Sanders P (1993) *An Incomplete Guide to Using Counselling Skills on the Telephone*, PCCS Books

Suler J (1997) *The Black Hole of Cyberspace* (blog entry), May: http://users.rider.edu/~suler/psycyber/blackhole.html [Our top tip: scroll down!]

Suler J (2004) 'The Online Disinhibition Effect', *CyberPsychology & Behavior*, Volume 7, Number 3, 2004: https://pdfs.semanticscholar.org/c70a/ae3be9d370ca1520db5edb2b326e3c2f91b0.pdf

Thompson R (2016) *Psychology at a Distance: Examining the Efficacy of Online Therapy* (university thesis), Portland State University: https://pdxscholar.library.pdx.edu/cgi/viewcontent.cgi?article=1343&context=honorstheses

Treanor A (2017) *The Extent to Which Relational Depth Can Be Reached in Online Therapy and the Factors that Facilitate and Inhibit That Experience: A Mixed Methods Study* (doctoral thesis): https://pure.roehampton.ac.uk/portal/en/studentTheses/the-extent-to-which-relational-depth-can-be-reached-in-online-the and https://drive.google.com/file/d/1iVG5hTsy3P131PKLpVUA WTkT0W6pr2KF/view

Trebilcock O (2020) '*Headphones: how* much do they really harm your hearing?', *Which?:* https://www.which.co.uk/news/2020/03/headphones-how-much-do-they-really-harm-your-hearing/

Zamania Z, Nasira R & Yusooff F (2010) 'Perceptions towards online counseling among counselors in Malaysia', *Procedia Social and Behavioral Sciences*, 5, 585–589: https://core.ac.uk/download/pdf/82549415.pdf

Index

Printed in Great Britain
by Amazon

58643388R00118